CLASSIC TALES OF LIFE OUTDOORS

The Great Lakes Seasons Trilogy

More than eighty top outdoor
and nature writers share favorite tales
of life in the woods, fields, and waters
of the Upper Great Lakes Region.
Select the *Seasons* collection from
your home state, or check out all three.
Each book reflects the distinct
landscape and literary character
of its state. Each will evoke memories
of your own favorite haunts and
enhance your enjoyment of the
outdoors. All deserve a special place
beside the fireplace, or on the shelf
at your vacation getaway.

The Cabin
Bookshelf

1234 Hickory Drive ▪ Waukesha, WI 53186

CLASSIC TALES OF LIFE OUTDOORS

Wisconsin Seasons

FEATURING WRITINGS BY:

Richard Behm

Scott Bestul

Gary Busha

Tom Davis

Roger Drayna

Mel Ellis

R. Chris Halla

Sharon Hart Addy

Dion Henderson

Steve Hopkins

Justin Isherwood

Don Johnson

Tom Joseph

Jack Kulpa

Aldo Leopold

Leroy Lintereur

Gordon MacQuarrie

Doug McLean

John Motoviloff

Chuck Petrie

Jay Reed

Bob Riepenhoff

Clay Schoenfeld

Dan Small

Bill Stokes

George Vukelich

Jerry Wilber

Galen Winter

Dick Yatzeck

CLASSIC TALES OF LIFE OUTDOORS

Wisconsin Seasons

Edited by
Ted J. Rulseh

Illustrated by
Sharon Anderson

Front cover photo by
Bob Rashid

Back cover photo by
Bill Kinney

The Cabin
Bookshelf

1234 Hickory Drive ■ Waukesha, WI 53186

WISCONSIN SEASONS
Classic Tales of Life Outdoors
Edited by Ted J. Rulseh

Wisconsin Seasons
Classic Tales of Life Outdoors
© 1998 by The Cabin Bookshelf

Front cover photograph © Bob Rashid. Reprinted by permission.
Back cover photograph by Bill Kinney, Ridgeland, Wis.
Reprinted by permission.

Interior illustrations ©1998 by Sharon Anderson, Iola, Wis.

Text and cover design ©1998 Tamara L. Dever, Orangevale, Calif.

Publisher's Cataloging in Publication
        (Prepared by Quality Books, Inc.)

Wisconsin seasons: classic tales of life outdoors/edited by Ted Rulseh;
        illustrated by Sharon Anderson. — 1st ed.
        p. cm.
        ISBN: 0-9653381-5-0

        1. Hunting–Wisconsin–Anecdotes.   2. Fishing–Wisconsin–
Anecdotes.   3. Outdoor life–Wisconsin–Anecdotes.   I.
Rulseh, Ted.

SK143.W57 1998   799'.09775
                             QBI98-662

Library of Congress Catalog Card Number: 98-70618

DEDICATION

To Noelle, Sonya, Todd and Nisse.

They know who they are

and why this book is for them.

TED J. RULSEH
April 1998

TABLE OF CONTENTS

FOREWORD *by Ted J. Rulseh*
page XV

xiii

CONTENTS, CONTINUED

FOREWORD

When I began seeking contributions to my first Wisconsin outdoor writing anthology (*Harvest Moon*, 1993), one of the first writers to respond was George Vukelich. That amazed me: he was one of the top writers in the state, and I was just some guy with a wild idea and a decent-looking letterhead. But here it was, a Tuesday, three days after I mailed letters to some hundred and fifty writers, and George Vukelich himself was on the phone, offering me rights to his deer hunting story "Coming of Age." I accepted, of course.

Another top writer, Clay Schoenfeld, was just as gracious. When I phoned for permission to reprint his story "Chasing Rainbows," he effused about what an honor it was to be included and tried hard to turn down the modest payment I offered.

In truth, I was the one who deserved to feel honored to have both men in *Harvest Moon*, and I am honored once again to have them in this new collection, *Wisconsin Seasons*. I only regret, as many readers do, that we must now call them "the late," along with Mel Ellis, Aldo Leopold, Dion Henderson and Gordon MacQuarrie, whose works also appear on these pages.

I encountered Vukelich through "North Country Notebook," his column in the Madison weekly *Isthmus*. The first time I read the column, I could almost feel my pulse slow down, much as it does when I arrive for a vacation at a Northwoods cabin and sit for a while on the lakefront porch, watching the loons and slowly rigging my fishing rods.

Vukelich may have lived in Madison, but his was a Northwoods soul, and his words carried the swish and scent of wind through tall pines. More than any writer, he *was* the North. To this day, I can hardly fish for bluegills without replaying his column about his father's canepoles, "long as a city block"; can hardly hear mention of Three Lakes without thinking of Steady Eddy and the gang sitting around at the American Legion Bar, "turning wine into water."

Schoenfeld was held in high esteem not just as a writer and author but as journalist, university administrator and conservationist. I remember him mainly for his book *Down Wisconsin Sideroads*, a Christmas present from my parents some years ago. I still keep *Sideroads* on the living room shelves — never stuffed it into a box in the basement with the texts and assorted paperbacks I accumulated during and after college.

To Schoenfeld, sideroads were an attitude, a way of living. If we drive from Madison to Milwaukee on the backroads instead of the freeway, he wrote, we won't get there "so fast or so smoothly," but we may have a chance, on a certain spring day, to "watch the swallows swarm back to their mud apartments on the side of a red barn ... " That's a thought worth remembering, wherever we may be going, in whatever season.

Perhaps fittingly, the Vukelich and Schoenfeld pieces included here are among their last writings — pieces they submitted themselves back in 1994, especially for this book. I'm pleased to present them as mementos of their writing careers, and as reminders that their works are still available, still worth seeking out.

I am also honored to bring back, for the first time between covers, the work of the late Leroy Lintereur, a former northeast district wildlife manager for the Wisconsin Department of Natural Resources. For many years, Lintereur's nature column was a fixture in the Marinette newspaper, and his keen observations helped draw his readers a little closer to the world around them.

May this second Wisconsin anthology draw us all, in some small way, a little closer to the woods, fields, lakes, streams and sideroads of our home state.

Ted J. Rulseh, Publisher
The Cabin Bookshelf
April 1998

Winter has loosed its hold,

and you are alive with the thought of it.

You leave your work and walls to swim

the spawning trails of spring.

It's a fine day for walking,

in this in-between time, when tentacles

of snow cling to shadows, when it's

too late for fishing and too early.

JERRY WILBER
From "Maybe Tomorrow"

Gary Busha

Growing up in the 1950s and living on Lake Winnebago were important elements in shaping Gary Busha's view of the world. Fishing was an integral part of his life. "Today the old house is gone," says Gary, "and the fishing is nothing like it was. Yet I'll never forget the wonderful years I spent there, fishing, skiffing the mysterious marsh, and putting in the dock every April." Today, Gary and family live in Sturtevant, Wis., near Racine. Gary writes poetry and fiction and has been published in hundreds of small-press magazines. He is publisher of Wolfsong Publications, a small press devoted mostly to poetry. He is self-employed with a writing and editorial business.

Reprinted by permission of the author. This story first appeared in Bachy 11, *published in 1978 by Papa Bach Paperbacks; it was reprinted in 1996 in Page 5.*

Putting In the Dock

GARY BUSHA

Time for a break. Our feet tingle
as they warm; our pockets are filled
with bolts and washers; a crescent wrench
sticks out of one of my pockets;
the smell of warm biscuits fills the house.

arly April, when the ice had broken up and all chance of a heavy freeze was gone, it was time for putting in the dock. Four sections with a larger platform for the end, the dock was numbered with lumber crayon so that each section went in the same, year after year. The iron cross braces were numbered, too, and in some cases, only certain bolts would fit through certain section holes. Putting in the dock was partly a matter of matching the numbers.

Three of us put in the dock. I'm the one wearing the heavy parka, hip boots that reach almost to my waist, and wire-rimmed glasses. I'm the one with the bleary eyes. Behind the short stub of an unlit, factory seconds cigar, powerfully built with bright blue eyes, is my dad. He's the one wearing waders that come up to the middle of his chest. He's the one who picks up the sixteen-pound maul as if it were a toothpick. Behind him is Grampa, unsteady, round-shouldered, the one with the short pipe in his mouth, wearing full bib overalls. He is seventy-three, and he holds a carpenter's level in his hand. Today is the tenth of April, and we are putting in the dock.

First we bolt the cross brace to the first section. Dad pulls the first dock section out while Grampa and I slip the bolts and washers in. The cold April wind whips waves up, and sometimes the big rollers slosh over Dad's waders. He sets the bolts through the cross brace. I walk out on the section with a maul and tap the posts down. Grampa brings the carpenter's level; he finds the section all out of kilter, and Dad readjusts the cross brace. Sometimes a few good taps with the maul will straighten her out.

It's the same procedure for the next section, and the next, except the water gets deeper, and the waves are more likely to slosh over the waders. My hip boots are only good for the first couple of sections, where the water is not so deep. I duck under the dock and tighten the bolts.

Time for a break. Hot coffee, warm biscuits, a fresh cigar, talk of the weather. We all agree it will be a good fishing year. Our feet tingle as they warm; our pockets are filled with bolts and washers; a crescent wrench sticks out of one of my pockets; the smell of warm biscuits fills the house.

"Getting in the platform will be the dickens," Grampa says as he draws heavily on his pipe. Dad and I nod in agreement. It's the same every year. We look out the large bay window after a strong gust of wind scatters some small branches against it. Time to get the rest of it in.

With Dad in the water and Grampa and me each holding an end of the platform, we move her out to the last section and bolt her in place. The platform, awkward and heavy, is the toughest to maneuver. Once she's in, leveled and bolted, I know our job is almost done. All that remains is to set the railings and bolt down the bench.

As we come back into the house, I'm the one whose teeth are chattering. Each year it's the same. We all go to the big bay window and look out to admire the dock.

"Looks real sturdy and level this year," Dad says.

"It's a dickens of a job," Grampa says.

I shiver and look back toward the kitchen, where the table is piled with hot, steaming food.

Scott Bestul *is a Wisconsin native whose ties to the Badger state remain strong. He and his wife, Shari, live in southeastern Minnesota, and the pair frequently border-hop the Mississippi River, hunting or fishing whichever state feels right that day. Scott learned to deer hunt on family land near Iola, the setting for the accompanying story. He is an avid deer, turkey and upland game bird hunter and spends his summers fly fishing for muskies, smallmouth bass, and trout. Scott's writing has appeared in a number of state, regional and national outdoor magazines, and he is currently a regional editor for* Field & Stream. *He also edited the outdoor writing anthology* Minnesota Seasons.

Redemption Gobbler

SCOTT BESTUL

Armed with a vestful of calls and more
experience than my cousin, I want
desperately to bring a gobbler to his gun.
In a couple of seasons, I know,
he won't need me. Today, I feel a gnawing
desire to shine for him in the
only area I feel capable.

I've had wild turkeys gobble so close to me I reached up to hold my hat in place, and I've listened to gobbles so distant I thought they were yesterday's memories. But the deep, throaty *Robble-Robble Gil-lobble!!* that now caroms off the oaks seemed the sweetest turkey talk I've ever heard. Cousin Scott and I listen, eyes to the ground and ears cocked at the horizon.

"Sound like two?" he asks, shifting a pair of high-brass shotshells in his gloved palm.

"At least. Maybe three," I guess.

"Which side of the creek do you think they're on?"

"Not ours, I bet."

We grin and nod knowingly. Murphy and his law are so much a part of our hunts we've come to embrace him like a friend. The toms fall silent for several minutes. We wait patiently for the gobbling to resume so we can pinpoint the roost and cut the distance without spooking them. The April woods, jarred by the predawn gobbling, awaken grudgingly. A raven coughs. Songbirds warble tentatively. Scott finally gives the leaves a gentle kick and turns to me.

"Hoot at 'em. We should get a better bearing on them, don't you think?"

I nod and swallow. Gathering a deep breath, I rush air out of my lungs into hollow jowls and pursed lips. A shrill "Whooorlll ... !" rolls through the woods. The call is my one-note rendition of the barred owl Who-Cooks-for-You sequence. It's a well-known quirk of the male turkey to respond to barred owls, and their easily imitated hooting is a standard locator call. The owl song has barely died before the toms respond, their shrill gobbles interrupting each other. Scott chuckles softly, points without hesitation at the creek, and reaches for the Browning leaning nearby.

"Geez. You didn't have to get 'em that worked up, did ya?" I shrug and smile, then pat my vest nervously, making sure my calls are in place. An old, rutted logging trail provides a convenient path toward the gurgling creek we've picked as our landmark. As we walk, sweat beads on my forehead and my jaws grind tighter. It's a familiar ague, one I get often when calling turkeys for clients, family and friends. Pregame jitters. The only time I've felt anything close is at the starting line of cross-country races in high school and college. But turkeys are the newer, and stronger, catalyst for the bug.

Scott's presence normally would calm me, but today it doesn't, an uncomfortable truth I'm trying to shake off. Not only do we share the same name, but we've been best friends and hunting companions for nearly twenty years. Our wives and mutual friends accept as fate our identical monikers; our personalities, even our thoughts, are so similar we could have been twins. Lately, however, I've wrestled with the uncomfortable notion that there is some hero worship in my feelings for Scott. While outsiders see us as partners, I feel a hint of envy, an emotion I've struggled to control.

On a logical plane, I can talk myself out of this. Our overall take of game — what we jokingly call "the body count" — is similar. Our woodsmanship and hunting ability are fairly even. But deep inside I feel Scott has a confidence I long for but may never possess. New skills come easily for him; I struggle to match his ease and thrift in the woods. It's not easy, I half kid myself, battling the sidekick complex, always wanting to be like Scott Bestul.

I work to dismiss these thoughts as we approach the roost. Despite his prowess, Scott has yet to tag a turkey, and I, armed with a vestful of calls and more experience than my cousin, want desperately to bring a gobbler to his gun. In a couple of seasons, I know, he won't need me. Today I feel a gnawing desire to shine for him in the only area I feel capable.

Thankfully, the toms are doing their best to help. The sun is warming the woods, and the birds must feel it on their breasts, as well. Each minute their gobbles increase in intensity, and before we reach the creek it is obvious the turkeys are on the other side. Turkey hunting fundamentalists preach incessantly about removing obstacles like water, ditches and fencelines from a bird's path when calling. Such snags can cause a tom to "hang up," make him pace in front of a jam he could cross with a simple flap of his wings — if only he wanted to. Scott knows this and turns to me, his brow deeply furrowed.

"I suppose we should get on their side of the creek. Or would they cross it?"

"They might," I whisper. "But I'd love to get over there. How far do they seem to

you?"

Turkey hunters know this question is not one query but three, and is so loaded it's spontaneously combustible. Calling, camo, shooting, all are kid stuff next to Where-Are-the-Birds, What's-Between-Us,   How-Close-Can-We-Get-Without-Spooking-Them? "A hundred yards. Maybe one-fifty," Scott replies evenly. He knows these woods so well I never think of questioning him. Visualizing the distance, I scuff the ground beneath my boot. Chalkboard dry and full of twigs. When I glance at Scott his scowl indicates the leaves are too dry for further sneaking.

"Better not risk bumping them. We'll just call them across," I whisper hoarsely. The toms continue their frantic gobbling and, just as we select a pair of trees to lean against, I hear three distinct fly-downs. The birds are close, the terrain flat, and I've almost convinced myself we can coax them over the water when a croaky yelping joins the chorus of gobbles. Scott mutters an obscenity and glares at me through his face mask. "Hen?"

I nod and mumble, "Strike two."

The presence of hens can hurt or help a turkey hunter, depending on the situation. In this case, I couldn't imagine anything worse. I pictured the distant toms, falling over their beards trying to impress the feathered minx before them. Their gobbling waned and I knew they were concentrating on strutting technique, showcasing their virility in a shimmering display of mahogany feathers and blood-engorged heads.

"That little tramp is leading them around by their beaks," I whisper to Scott.

He manages a grin. "What now?"

"Plan One is to sound bossier than she does and hope she comes over to clean house." I own enough turkey calls to supply a small store, but I rely on only a handful for the crisis turkey hunters label "henned-up toms." On a whim I reach for a long, thin-walled, aptly named box dubbed the Boat Paddle — a call looking like it could indeed propel a small canoe or duck boat. It also produces a squeaky, obnoxious grate that somehow drives turkeys wild. It's always dangerous surmising the whys of turkey vocabulary, but a Missouri friend who's an expert caller summed up the Boat Paddle's appeal far better than its manufacturer: "The thing burns their ears like a damn hot-plate."

I decide then, with the real hen yelping and purring merrily, to burn some turkey ears. I squeak out a couple of raspy yelps, pause, then string together an aggressive sequence known as "cutting."

Cutting is a call attributed to dominant hens, who use it to show excitement to toms or to demand respect from other females. That's the human interpretation of cutting, but then, this is a bird with a brain the size of a walnut. For all we know it could mean, "Here are some acorns! Big ones!" But the birds like the cutting. At least the toms do, and their urgent gobbling rolls off the trees. The hen is decidedly less enthusiastic. Her return cutting matches the Boat Paddle's and then some. I repeat the sequence, adding volume. The toms gobble in unison. The hen ups her vocals, and we hear her racing toward us through the leaves, popping and clucking. I motion to Scott to raise the gun, knowing the gobblers will follow, but just when I'm sure we'll see her, she retreats. I curse under my breath.

The yelping fades after the hen's frantic rush. She is leading the gobblers away from our position, wanting, I imagine, to eliminate any competition. The toms, typical males under the heavy influence of testosterone, will follow her mindlessly. Scott sighs deeply as the calling disappears, and I see his back sag against the tree. I long for the time, only minutes ago, when the creek was our biggest problem.

Scott turns and says plainly, "Any ideas?"

I squirm uncomfortably at the question. Scott asks for my opinion frequently while deer hunting, but I often feel it's a courtesy, a chance to get a second opinion on a decision he's already made. But in this instance he needs me to solve the problem, and I find it unnerving. I swallow dryly.

"We could reposition," I mumble. "Try 'em from another angle. Sometimes it works. Can we sneak out of here and make a short loop around them?"

Scott nods, rises, and starts a confident stalk. We retrace our steps through the woods, walk a field edge, and pop back into the timber, sneaking until we are at the creek bank again, but a hundred yards downstream. I follow in his footsteps contentedly. When we reach a large oak he turns to me.

"This what you had in mind?"

"Perfect," I reply. And it is. We're on a narrow oak ridge that leads directly to the stream. The ridge is full of fresh scratchings and droppings and, most important, the birds haven't heard a call here yet this morning. I reach for the Boat Paddle, then decide a new sound might turn the trick here. As Scott settles back against an oak, I reach into my vest for a cloth bag containing a call designed by my Missouri friend. Tad simply replaced the disc of slate with a layer of polished metal, and the yelps it produces are so high-pitched they ring through the woods. If the Boat Paddle burns a turkey's ears, this call chars them.

I wait for a couple of minutes, letting the woods settle, then rap out a series of yelps, high and quavering. At the first note Scott starts, then looks back at me. Even I'm surprised by the metallic, piercing calls, and I pray the birds will answer and prove I haven't ruined us.

I listen, holding my breath. Nothing. The gobblers had to have heard. For a panicked minute I picture them, shaking their heads uncomfortably and retreating from the grating yelps. As I might after a desperate, mistimed jump shot launched in a pickup basketball game, I wish only to be able to take the calls back, but it's too late. My only hope is to grab the rebound and take it hard to the hoop. Clutching the call in a death grip, I grind the striker against the shiny metal and bang out a series of yelps that slap my eardrums.

The woods erupt with turkey talk. The three toms answer frantically, their double- and triple-gobbles so eager Scott and I look at each other wide-eyed. The hen pops and cutts indignantly. I answer once more, softly, just to affirm our position. The birds sound off again, more ardent and slightly closer. And then the hunting gods deal us a huge trump card. A deep, throaty gobble sounds behind us — a fourth tom, attracted by the constant, intense calling, has entered the show. I shake my head in disbelief. In an instant we have gone from desperadoes to winning lotto ticket holders. Scott turns to me as Gobbler Four explodes again, gaining decibels by the second. I hold up a trigger finger and jerk it theatrically.

"Get ready," I whisper. "Things could happen fast now."

It turns out to be one of the few understatements I've been granted in my hunting career. We are surrounded by birds that lecherously, desperately, want to gather in our laps. The hen comes unglued. Or she just likes the sound of Gobbler Four's voice better. The Gobbler Trio follows the hen — or they prefer heavy metal yelping. Or they want to beat the stuffing out of the new boy on the block.

When you are in the midst of turkeys, all humping it toward you, you don't question the whys of their coming. You get your gun on your knee, concentrate on deep breathing, and anticipate a clear shooting lane. We hear their tromping through dry leaves. It is tough to tell which will reach us first. With an inexperienced hunter, I like to be right beside him at this time, whispering softly where to point the gun and when to fire. But I know this is unnecessary with Scott, who filters the fear out of adrenaline and turns the rush into keener vision, lucid thought.

In seconds I see three blue heads pop into view and glimpse Scott easing his gun barrel toward the largest tom. Gobbler Four gobbles immediately at the sound of the shot. Loud, sharp sounds will often make a tom do that, but the sight of two upright figures trotting toward a fallen turkey will always make his companions fly. The hen, two-thirds of the Trio, and Gobbler Four leave so quickly it seems, seconds later, that they had never been there at all. Scott and I whoop in unison when we reach the tom. It is magnificent. Its feathers, caught in the April sunlight, glow deep ebony, shining copper, burnished bronze, a kaleidoscope of iridescence. The white, turquoise and scarlet of the gobbler's head seemingly lift it from the carpet of oak leaves. I gawk at the bird in silence until Scott's voice breaks my stare.

"That call really brought 'em in, didn't it?"

I switch my gaze to the shiny metal disc in my hand and laugh.

"Yeah. This thing really wakes up the woods."

But when I look up, Scott's eyes are on me, not the call.

"That was some good calling," he says. It is, I know, as nice a compliment as he offers, and I suddenly feel the warmth of the April sun on my back. We kneel by the bird for many minutes, replaying memories, stroking feathers. When the stories come to an end, Scott tags the bird and slings it over his shoulder. He starts toward the truck, but I linger for a moment, gathering my gear, casing the metal call and the hickory striker in their little bag. I know I'll never be certain what brought the turkeys in so suddenly. But I do know that, at this moment, my best friend feels I've come up big, and for the first time in many months it's okay being Scott Bestul again.

Tom Davis *lived in Door County for nearly fourteen years before moving to Green Bay, where he is settling into his role as a suburban stepdad. "I'm not really sure whether I'm a parent or a valet," he says, "although I have no doubt as to my stepdaughter's opinion on the matter." Well known in the state for his work in* Wisconsin Trails *magazine ("I seem to have an uncanny knack for inciting rage among our genteel readership"), Tom also enjoys a national following as senior editor of* Sporting Classics, *editor-at-large of* Pointing Dog Journal, *and author of such books as* Just Goldens *and* The Little Book of Flyfishing. *He is also known in certain circles as "the Fool of the Brule," though that is not a title he necessarily embraces.*

Reprinted by permission of the author.
This selection first appeared in Gray's Sporting Journal.

The Toothsome Pike-Perch

TOM DAVIS

There's something fulfilling about sliding
the net beneath a walleye, something that
nourishes a hungry soul. With other fish,
I don't mind long-distance releases.
Walleye, I want to possess.
They bring out the greed in me.

This was strange. A light breeze pulsed from the southwest, and we drifted with it at a perfect angle over the sunken reef. As soon as we felt our jigs tick the slope of the reef, one of us — or both — had a fish on. I'd net Dad's fish, or he'd net mine, and I'd thread it on the stringer. Then I'd yank the five-horse Evinrude to life, and we'd circle back into position for the next drift. The stringer was filling nicely.

But when we glanced over our right shoulders as we rhythmically worked the jigs, we saw something coming. A squall line hove in from the north, its leading edge like cotton balls swabbed through the barrel of a dirty gun. The clouds were dark and roiling and ominous, and advancing at a menacing pace. What was strange was that the wind was still blowing from the opposite direction. Clearly, this was not good. Prudence dictated that we get off the water; appetite, and willing fish, persuaded us to stay.

Finally the center of the lake went dead calm. The sky assumed a peculiar greenish cast. The air thickened. We could see the waves at the north end of the lake break back against themselves. Then, as if it were subject to the laws of plate tectonics, the whole surface seemed to shift and rearrange into two converging halves, with us at the seam. I opened the throttle as wide as it would go and pointed the dinghy for home. The little Evinrude will purr along at trolling speed for hours, but it won't get you anywhere in a hurry. An eighth of a mile and a small eternity later, we looked back to see a waterspout materialize at precisely the place we'd just exited. I'm not saying it would have clean-and-jerked us off the water, but it would have spun us like a bottle, not to mention scaring the hell out of us. The heavens opened as I skidded the boat onto shore, and we sprinted to the house in a blinding rain, lightning cracking all around.

So, there we were, risking life and limb, for what? Bull-shouldered, acrobatic smallmouth? Line-peeling, reel-smoking northerns? Heavy, intractable lake trout? Wrong on all counts. We were catching pound-and-a-half walleyes, fish that fought feebly if at all. And we were loving it.

Across a broad swatch of the country's belly, the average, semi-serious angler is walleye-crazy. What brookies are to New England, largemouth bass to the South and rainbows to the West, walleyes are to the North Central states. They are not just quarry. They are an object of desire.

And yet, when you stop to analyze it, the walleye's appeal is elusive. Most simply take it as a given. Certainly, there is no better table fish. You can get all epicurean and esoteric, talk Norwegian salmon and mahi-mahi and Dover sole, but the sweet, white, flaky flesh of walleye renders all arguments moot. The walleye's eating qualities were the inspiration behind my favorite fish sobriquet, dreamed up long ago by some earnest hook-and-bullet writer who, like most hook-and-bullet writers, delighted in substituting descriptive epithets for proper names. This forgotten soul called the walleye "the toothsome pike-perch."

Toothsome as in morsel (not wench), and suggestive of the walleye's impressive dentition; pike-perch as a nod to the colloquial "walleyed pike" and to its membership in the perch family. In my opinion, the toothsome pike-perch beats the hell out of "ol' marble eyes," which puts me in mind of a blinded Sinatra.

These days, however, few of us fish just to eat. We cast our lures upon the waters for the sport of it, and in sporting terms the walleye grades out poorly.

"God's most boring fish," one friend sniffs.

"Overgrown baitfish," sneers another.

The tragic truth is that walleyes don't fight worth a damn. In the piscatorial ring, walleyes are the white guys. They're slow, sluggish, and rarely last through the first round. Even a half-dead, spawned-out salmon puts up a nobler struggle. Occasionally, a walleye will strike a crankbait with uncommon authority. But in the usual walleye fishing scenario — still-fishing with a slip bobber and live bait, drifting a jig-and-minnow, trolling a spinner-and-leech — the take is nearly imperceptible, and to call what ensues a fight is to be obscenely generous.

What makes the walleye's allure even more curious is the abundance, in walleye country, of other species that are both bigger and stronger. I know sportsmen who make an annual fly-in trip to the Ontario wilderness. The lake they fish teems with leg-long northerns, which they utterly ignore in order to concentrate on two- to four-pound walleyes. Minnesota's Leech Lake, site of the legendary Muskie Uprising of 1955, was discovered to be a muskie hotspot only after the walleye fishing declined to the point that local guides were forced to explore alternatives. There are chinook salmon, steelhead, and brown trout that grow to thirty pounds in the Great Lakes. The fiercest battler of all, the smallmouth bass, occupies many of the same habitats as the walleye. All are incomparably superior fighters, and only the smallmouth doesn't exceed the walleye in average size. Yet the toothsome pike-perch would win a popularity test hands down.

You have to acknowledge that there is a kind of coarse beauty to this fish. Its lines are smooth and tapered — some might even say troutlike. Color is where the walleye really shines: depending on the tint of the water, it can range from bright yellow to burnished gold to rich amber. The walleyes from the Berens Rivers system of Manitoba, where the water runs the color of bourbon, are gorgeous. In the northern light, their flanks burn red.

One school of thought holds that the walleye is the "common man's trout." This analogy hinges partly on both trout and walleye being wary, presentation-sensitive fish that pose a challenge and require an advanced level of skill to hook. The implied white-collar (trout)–blue-collar (walleye) distinction, however, doesn't hold up. Plenty of executives have tricked-out Lunds in their garages, and lots of clock-punchers own Orvis products.

But the challenge doesn't explain the spell walleyes cast over anglers any more than looks do. Ultimately, I think this spell is a racial memory, an atavistic remnant from an era when fishing was far more food-oriented than it is today. For most of this century, people fished to enjoy themselves — but also to fill the freezer. A full stringer of fish was a symbol of Man the Provider, a Rockwellian icon. And if it was a stringer of walleyes, the best-tasting fish in the land, so much the better. A man who could present his wife a limit of walleyes felt like a hero. Sons sought to emulate fathers, and even as the original reasons for the walleye's pre-eminence faded, the peculiar satisfaction associated with landing a respectable walleye persisted. The advent of catch-and-release has not altered this.

Of course, the walleye predilection is as mysterious to those in its thrall as any other inherited (or unconsciously acquired) appetite. There's just something fulfilling about sliding the net beneath a walleye, something that nourishes a hungry soul. There's a sense of accomplishment. It feels good. With other fish, I don't mind long-distance releases. Walleye, I want to *possess*. They bring out the greed in me. I'm not a hog by any means, but I might be a bit of a piglet.

It was inevitable, I suppose that walleye fishing would be infected by the viruses of science and technology. A quarter-century ago, when I started out, it was a pretty simple game. You fished when they were biting, where they were biting. In spring and early summer, you could catch walleyes in the resort belt of Wisconsin and Minnesota; come midsummer, you had to head for Canada and cooler water. There was a nice symmetry to it.

Techniques and equipment were very basic as well. You trolled. In the States, this normally meant a spinner-and-minnow rig; in Canada, you snapped a Flatfish or Lazy Ike behind a bead-chain sinker. Those who fished with jigs were considered on the cutting edge. Rapalas were new on the scene and were used more or less experimentally.

Then along came Al Lindner, to mention only the most prominent of the walleye prophets, with this revolutionary notion that you could hook walleyes when and where you wanted to, that you weren't constrained by calendar or geography. This was heady stuff. It stood convention on its head. Lindner and his disciples contended that the secret lay in recognizing and adjusting to changes in the fish's behavior. These changes could be triggered by any number of combinations of stimuli

Eventually, this gospel was refined into an elaborate, interconnected theory of "patterns." There is a pre-spawn pattern and a post-spawn pattern. There are midsummer, late summer and fall patterns. Reservoirs have different patterns from natural lakes, which have different patterns from rivers. Canadian Shield lakes have unique patterns as well. Clear water, dirty water and stained water all have their own patterns. There are patterns for wood, weeds and rocks; patterns for fish in negative, neutral and aggressive modes. There are live-bait patterns and patterns for artificials; daytime patterns and nighttime patterns; patterns for the full of the moon and for the dark of the moon.

It gets extremely intricate and complicated. Needless to say, the contemporary walleye specialist is a master of a language as dense and incomprehensible to the casual angler as that of the most entomologically-enslaved trouter. Quite a bit of useful information has trickled down to non-denominational fishermen like me, information that has increased our knowledge and improved our catches.

But, sadly, there has come the predictable union of religion and business. If you do not buy in, literally and figuratively, you are considered unworthy, impure, an infidel. The implication is that you cannot possibly enjoy yourself unless you keep the faith. When you read the manifestos — or when you watch the televangelists, who are only slightly less histrionic than Hulk Hogan — you realize that this is not walleye fishing as you have known it, but something colossal, something out of proportion, an obsession with methodology for its own sake. Its link to what we call sport is buried under an avalanche of dogma.

Me, I'm at peace with my ignorance. My approach to walleye fishing is low-tech, low-brow, and old-fashioned. About the first of May, I haul the twelve-foot fiberglass dinghy out of the shed, hose it down and sponge it off. A relative paid a hundred bucks for it; if you lift up the front seat (a carpeted trapezoid of plywood), you see "Irreg" stamped on the hull. Part of the port gunwale is caved in, the result of mooring the boat on the wrong side of the dock during a storm, so every spring I cover the damage with a neat, new layer of duct tape. Every third spring, I take the Evinrude in to be tuned up. It's of early 1960s vintage and as reliable as they come. It smokes more than a little, but I can throttle it down to a crawl that drives walleyes mad. No, I don't own an electric trolling motor, a fish locator, or any other badge of sophistication.

The lake I fish is about a thousand acres, and shallow. The walleyes do not run big. Five pounds is the largest I've heard of, four pounds the heaviest I personally claim, although three-and-a-half is probably nearer the mark. The lake does enjoy a reputation for particularly succulent walleyes, a reputation that my experience bears out.

Still, with Lake Michigan on one side and Green Bay on the other, angling pressure is negligible. You will hear nothing of this lake on the local radio's fishing reports, and if you ask the owners of the area's best-known tackle shop about it, you will put them at a disadvantage. Or they will wonder aloud why you'd bother fishing for the occasional small walleye, when you could be wrangling with bruisers out on Green Bay.

These guys are Salesmen with a capital S. I'm convinced they apprenticed in previous lives as carnival barkers and purveyors of patent medicines. A few years back, I stopped into the store to replenish my supply of marabou jigs. I searched the displays in vain for what I thought was a standard item. One of the partners asked if he could help. I told him what I wanted, and he asked, "What are you fishing for?"

"Walleyes," I replied, innocently.

"Here's what you need for walleyes," he announced, and started handing me bubble cards with chartreuse grub-body jigs sealed inside. Now, I know that many widely traveled walleye fishermen swear by chartreuse. I've even heard a respected Missouri guide, when questioned about colors for walleye, respond, "Any color, as long as it's chartreuse." Trouble is, the walleyes in my lake don't read or watch TV. Chartreuse gives them lockjaw. I tried to explain this to the Salesman, but he was loose, in stride, rockin' and rollin'. Powerless, I purchased the chartreuse grub-body jigs and scurried away.

The story improves. A few weeks after this encounter, a writer for a nearby newspaper drove up to fish with me. As we rigged our lines, I recounted the incident, assuming he would find it humorous. He remained impassive, a stone. Then he reached into the front pocket of his jacket and produced a bubble card containing chartreuse grub-body jigs.

"I think these will work," he huffed.

I just shrugged and landed three nice walleyes in a half-day of tough fishing, using a yellow marabou jig. My guest didn't catch squat, although he did, at last, abandon chartreuse.

I'm told that some people who fish this lake troll Rapalas successfully, but it's never panned out for me. I stick to marabou jigs — yellow mostly, sometimes black, or white, or white with a pink head — tipped with a fathead minnow. My usual procedure is to troll in lazy ellipses between the white frame boathouse and the cottage with the fieldstone patio, staying on the outside edge of the bulrushes. There are some rock humps out there, a bona fide reef or two, and a wooden fish crib dropped long ago by the DNR. If the wind's from the south, I'll drift this stretch and troll back. When I catch a walleye, I toss out a yellow buoy to mark the spot. You might think it would be more effective, once the school is located, to anchor and cast, or deploy slip bobbers. It's not (slip bobbers are too hard to rig, anyway). I do better simply trolling, shrouded in the blue smoke of the Evinrude, adjusting the tackle box and minnow bucket so they don't vibrate, gently bouncing the jig-and-minnow across the bottom.

I have an archaic formula that tells me when to start fishing. It goes like this: when the morels and wild asparagus appear, the walleyes begin to bite. This happy coincidence yields some of the premier suppers of the year: golden, pan-fried walleye fillets, morels dusted in flour and sauteed in butter, asparagus anointed with velvety Hollandaise. Cholesterol be damned.

The fishing lasts longer than the morels, but not by much. The action slows considerably about the middle of June. Rather than force the issue, I adopt a "to everything, there is a season" attitude. The walleye season on this lake is over by the first of July, so I turn my attention to other, more rewarding pursuits. Another May will come.

The hour before sunset is magic. You hear music hidden in the pitch of the outboard. It fills the air. It surrounds you. The thickly ranked cedars seem dusted with gold, and as the light slants, intensifying the shadows, their three-dimensionality appears heightened, as if you are looking through a stereoscope. Out of nowhere, out of somewhere, bats materialize, plucking caddis flies inches from the water. Wood ducks, square-tailed, erect-headed silhouettes, hug the treetops en route to secret ponds ringed by ancient hemlocks. In the abandoned orchards, a few hopeful woodcock still sing.

It feels right to fish walleyes here, the lights of the cottages blinking on, the light of day spilling into night. It is fishing as your father knew it, and your grandfather, fishing that is quiet and hopeful and fervent, and as important as it should be. Between fish, you troll the waters of your thoughts. Most of what you catch are eating-size at best, worthy of a chew or two. But you know, in the chambers of your heart, that trophies swim there, too, and with luck and patience they will be yours.

John Motoviloff *writes an outdoor column, "Driftless Notes," for the* Wisconsin River Valley Journal. *He and his wife, Kerry, own a cabin in the heart of the Driftless Country on the Kickapoo River. When not trout fishing, duck hunting, looking for mushrooms, or standing over a smoking grill in his East Madison backyard trying a new game marinade, John works as a production manager for the Journal Division of the University of Wisconsin Press. His poetry and essays have appeared in national publications. He is working on two books:* Driftless Stories, *a collection of outdoor essays; and* Portage, *a novel about deer hunting in the Midwest.*

Nightfall on a Trout Stream

JOHN MOTOVILOFF

*I rubbed the willow roots to confirm
my faith in the spot. You cannot
catch trout in the long run without faith.*

Below the shade tree, the big spring slipped toward the creek. A chill descended from the ridges, and the sky's windbreaker colors mellowed to blotched evening. I left the bridge, with its small trout, for the root tangle, walking through tall grass and honeysuckle. My tippet was too thin for worming in those tight quarters, but I didn't change it. The farmhouse windows were already yellow against the twilight.

The line swung beneath the elm roots as I knelt on the mud bank. Wood, water and undergrowth made the air thick to breathe; willows lined the banks, their bark like cardboard. To my right a forked stick was planted Tom Sawyer style. A farm kid, I thought. How often they find their mark, filling Wonder Bread bags with morels, dragging leg-sized trout home on bicycles.

I rubbed the willow roots to confirm my faith in the spot. You cannot catch trout in the long run without faith. Shadows fell from basswoods, maples and birches. My neck felt bare without my bandana. I thought of the walk back in the dark, picturing each fallen tree so I wouldn't twist my ankle. The waxy fly line hung against the current. Night kept coming on, blurring now into one solid shadow.

The line jumped between my thumb and index finger as I drew it taut, bounced like a tightrope walked on by a fat man. The rod bent slowly to half-moon; I dug my knees into the mud. Tight line in hand, I snapped the tip up — a solid trout, hooked well. But then I remembered the thin tippet.

Trying to be calm, I laid the net in the mud, rolled my sleeves and let him swim, let the darkness seal up the watery world until there was only the patina of the creek, a trout bull-dogging upstream and downstream. But then it hit me: I had the whole night if that's what it took. The heart pounding stopped. I smelled the cool mud and listened to night unfold. Natural as breath came prayer.

God, keep me when I have lost my way, keep me among woodlands and rivers. And as wildfowl know their way, even from the instinct of being, keep me fast to the good and beautiful.

The slap of a tail in the eddy broke the silence. He had tired, and I slid him onto the mud bank. A glowing slab of parchment. A pot-bellied German brown. The sound of cartilage on driftwood and then quiet, the echo of responsibility. I walked back as in a house known by contour. Cleaning the fish beneath the bridge in the yellow farm light, I said the prayer again, mouthing each word carefully.

Roger Drayna, *has been a freelance writer for nearly half a century. He sold the first of his 150 published articles while a junior at Superior State College in 1951. Writing for Roger "is like a crick in the neck. I just have to work it out." Mostly, his themes deal with the outdoors. You would expect that from someone who has canoed all over Wisconsin, in Maine and Washington, in the cypress swamps of Texas, in the Everglades, and across the Quetico wilderness of Ontario. Ten summers working for the U.S. Forest Service and as a seasonal ranger with the National Park Service got him close to nature in fair weather and foul. In 1954 he began his career teaching English and history in Antigo. In 1992 he retired after 24 years as a writer and as public relations director for Wausau Insurance. He lives in Wausau.*

The Gatherer

ROGER DRAYNA

Several miles cross-country,
a spring bursts, icy cold and gin-clear,
from among the roots of white cedars.
I never hesitate to kneel on the wet carpet
of forest debris, plunge my face into it,
and gulp. My face tingles, my lips
go numb, and there is a momentary
aching in my teeth. On a hot July
afternoon, these are rewards.

*I*t's difficult to recall how my collection got started. It could hardly be called acquisitiveness. Other than a desultory boyhood run at stamp collecting, a Navajo rug and Hopi pot from our Southwestern days, and my father's baptismal certificate executed in Cyrillic script, there is not much of the pack rat in me.

It did get started, I guess, behind the Pattison. If that doesn't strike you with household familiarity, you need not fear your education in Wisconsin geography has been neglected. Behind the Pattison was simply the whole province of fields and brushy woods stretching away from the back door of the Martin Pattison Elementary School. It has meaning only for kids who grew up in Superior from the late 1930s through the World War II years.

To the maternal inquiry, "Where are you going?" we would answer, "Behind the Pattison." These mothers, who thought it meant the playground or the baseball field, were stunned when, at last, they realized that behind the Pattison reached as far as the Nemidji River, a good four miles south of town.

It was a whole world of endless fascination, a place for boys to wander and wonder and learn and to cause parents to worry when we came straggling home after dark. Just thinking about it again calls up a flood of memories: ski trails, cackling pheasants (they fed on spilled Dakota grain in the railroad yards), boyhood traplines, and bacon fried to the verge of disintegration over a too-hot fire of tindery willow. There was even a bona fide Bum's Jungle in a scrubby popple glade at 28th Street and the Soo Line tracks. It was still active and sinister in those tag-end days of the Great Depression.

All of that, and more, is part of my collection. But what is most vivid is an early Saturday morning in November. I can picture myself still, hip-booted and knee-deep in an oozy-bottomed, ice-rimmed pothole, just lifting a large muskrat, very sodden and very rigid, from a drowning set. In 1945 its pelt would bring two and a half to three bucks. Hopalong Cassidy went for ten cents at the Palace Theater matinee. Even five decades later, I can sense the excitement, the nearness of affluence, as I dropped the muskrat into my pack.

At that very moment, high overhead, came the haunting voices of geese. I craned my neck to search for them. They were snows, maybe two hundred of them, mostly in one large, wavering vee, startlingly white against the vault of blue autumn sky, borne along by the rhythmic pumping of their black-tipped wings. In breathless reverence, I followed the receding white line as it dimmed in the distance. Then they were gone. Ever more faintly the barking continued. Then it, too, was gone.

The scene is burned into memory. The skinny kid trapper, the pond, the scraggly willows and popples already gone to the grayness of winter, the sky, and the geese. My geese. Forever my treasure. Far more valuable, I would understand later, than the lump of muskrat in my pack.

I can still find that pond and deliberately seek it out, now and then, when my travels take me to the Head-of-the-Lakes. It's not very impressive, less so since it is now hemmed in by an oil refinery, and offensive petroleum smells assault my nose as I push through the tall swamp vegetation to get a better look.

But it still speaks to me of solitude and bleak beauty and the love of wild places that awakened within me as I roamed the reaches of behind the Pattison.

Unlike the pond, which is mythical, most of my wild places remain beautiful, and I visit them now and again for what they promise of wilderness — even just a momentary glimpse of it. Along the headwaters of Douglas County's Bois Brule River, I can thread my canoe through gauntlets of Ice Age boulders where, close by each shoulder, ragged black spruce stab at the sky and cedars arch over the stream. There may be other canoes ahead or behind, but their sounds make me think only of the voyagers who once fought their way up this strong-willed river in search of the Northwest Passage. Aside from that, I hear nothing but the wind and the small sounds of flitting warblers; this could be an Alaskan river.

On clear days, heading west between Hurley and Ashland, there is a sweeping panorama just as U.S. 2 swoops down from Birch Hill. Away to the Northwest, beyond the forested miles of the Bad River Indian Reservation and the Kakogon Sloughs, Chequamegon Bay spreads itself in horizontal brightness, a sheet of hammered silver, merging at last with the vastness of Lake Superior. Beyond the bay, there is a rampart of hazy green, the backbone of the Bayfield Peninsula. It is one of the few places I can sense wilderness without even raising a sweat.

In Marinette County, a slanting ramp of granite juts out not far north of Highway 8. I hike it so I can sit in the warm April sun and consider tufts of moose moss holding to its coarse face, and jack pine seedlings jamming roots into crevices. Often, for the hawk migration is underway at that season, I'll watch a red-tail move in effortless circles, tip its wings, and slide away on the wind.

Several miles cross-country, a spring bursts, icy cold and gin-clear, from among the roots of white cedars. Although fishermen, coaxing brookies from beneath tangles of logs in K.C. Creek, pass within a hundred feet of it, I've never seen a human footprint in the soft, shadowy earth around it. There are few places these days where water is beyond the reach of the parasitic *Giardia lambia*. Still, nothing but sand hills and gravel ridges stretch away for miles in the direction from which this spring gathers its water. I never hesitate to kneel on the wet carpet of forest debris, plunge my face into it, and gulp. My face tingles, my lips go numb, and there is a momentary aching in my teeth. On a hot July afternoon, these are rewards.

Maxwell Spring in Langlade County is a place where brook trout, bellicose and aflame with color, begin to gather each October, answering the primordial command to perpetuate themselves. I try never to miss this celebration of species continuity. Not far from there, Woods Flowage, embraced by cedars and pinnacle-topped balsam firs, is good for thick-sided trout, warbler migrations, and spicy watercress to garnish a salad.

I must be a slow learner, because it took a couple of decades following these seasonal rites until I realized that I had put together an unusual collection. That idea just sort of emerged in my consciousness like dawn revealing a world of promise around our boyhood campsites. What it is, and continues to become, is my personal, custom-made wilderness, assembled from the places I have known and loved and which please me greatly.

Within its amorphous boundaries are hidden valleys where spring flowers carpet the hardwoods with incredible profusion. There are Lake Superior shorelines, sometimes placid, sometimes booming and groaning with heaving floe ice, and sometimes thundering with fearsome power. A towering moraine in Lincoln County is unfailing for sunsets, for facing a raw November wind, and for listening to the first hard snow crystals rattling among the russet curls of oak leaves.

Sometimes I give names to these places. One of these runs through our woods in the Harrison Hills, and only to me is it known as the Long Road. It leads me farther into the hills than any other.

The crown jewel of my collection is a Norway pine grove near the Michigan border. I first visited it back in 1952 when my wife's father, Neil Ramsay, hiked me to it. I had borrowed my dad's car to drive Marcy home from college. She had not yet agreed to trade in her sturdy Scottish surname, but I was working on it. The pines, about fifty of them, are hidden on a sandy flat enclosed by a U-shaped ridge, on eighty acres Neil had acquired two decades earlier. They are volunteers, which means, in the parlance of foresters, that they grew from seed wind-borne from a couple of really big Norways up the steep slope to the west. When I first saw them, they were not impressive, but Neil liked them, saw the promise they held. They were, perhaps, twenty feet tall then, five or six inches in diameter. Today they reach up almost a hundred feet, and I can barely get my arms around them.

The place was a favorite of Neil's, and over time it became a favorite of mine. He helped me build a crude little cabin among the pines. When our kids were little, Marcy and I would take them there for overnights. In spring, I can search out trailing arbutus hidden among layers of fallen needles. Later, delicate blue harebells nod in shafts of sunlight. Almost every year, a bear comes through, reaches as high as I can, and claws bark from the same tree — reasserting territorial rights.

Neil died in 1991, not far short of ninety. He was tall and lean and straight, like his trees. Almost to the last he loved to walk, and he did so with the easy grace of an athlete. In honesty and physical toughness, he was as uncompromising as these rugged hills and the Highlands of his forebears. A month or so after he died, I felt the need to visit his woods, and I struck off through the residual snow of March. Four miles later, in total solitude, I sat admiring his pines and thinking about him — the rivers we had paddled, the trout we had caught, and the grouse we sometimes tumbled out of swift flight. And, once again, I had a dawning experience. It came to me as I recalled Jim's Grove, a clump of Alpine fir right at the tree line, where climbers bivouac before taking on Long's Peak out in Rocky Mountain National Park. I knew, in that moment, that this hidden place, for me, would always be Neil's Grove. I played with the thought as I finished off the last of a thick meat sandwich and drained my Thermos bottle of coffee. Then I cinched up my pack and started the long walk back to warmth and companionship. Crossing the low ridge, I took another look at his pines. Neil's Grove. Perfect!

The Wilderness Act of 1964 was enlightened legislation, and its goal of sixty-one million acres preserved as true wilderness has now been exceeded. But we can get to such real wilderness only occasionally, if we are lucky. So I go about this business of gathering these small places where I can get the feel, if only briefly, of the wild, the unspoiled, and the lovely.

"Our ability to perceive quality in nature begins as in art, with the pretty," said Aldo Leopold. "It expands through successive stages of beautiful to values yet uncaptured by language."

That, I suppose, is the whole point. This collection is mine, because it moves me and satisfies me, because it is a part of what I am. Yet what is mine may be yours as well, for reasons known only to you. You may be moved by feelings deeper and more profound than mine.

The hundred million acres now designated as wilderness is an achievement. But, let us never forget the small triumphs like behind the Pattison and Neil's Grove. Their names are not on maps; their reality exists only in the consciousness of those who seek and cherish them.

Jerry Wilber *is a hunter, fisherman, wilderness camper, and professional fly tier who makes his base camp near South Range, Wis. He lives with wife Karen and daughter Katie on eighty wild acres "near Lake Superior and the mighty Brule River." Jerry is the author of two books,* ... of Woodsmoke and Quiet Places *(The Cabin Bookshelf, 1997) and* Wit & Wisdom of the Great Outdoors *(Pfeifer-Hamilton Publishers, 1993). His short stories have appeared in magazines throughout the United States and Canada, and his radio programs have been broadcast extensively across northwestern Wisconsin and northeastern Minnesota.*

Maybe Tomorrow

JERRY WILBER

*Just one more time I've got to ride
a canoe loaded with decoys, loaded with
distant skies, just the dog and me,
into the crispness of an October morning.
I've got to hear again the life-saving
sounds of mallards' wings.*

You are a feather falling from the sky, a fish shining in the water. You are an eagle playing with the wind and the yellow and orange and purple threads of dawn. Winter has loosed its hold, and you are alive with the thought of it.

There are things about this day too beautiful to lose, so you leave your books and business to walk into the birthing of the great out-of-doors. You leave your work and walls to swim the spawning trails of spring. It's a fine day for walking, in this in-between time, when tentacles of snow cling to shadows, when it's too late for really good fishing and too early.

On such days there's a war goes on inside you. Oh, not much of a war, a skirmish, maybe, but it's right there inside you finding the weak spots and pushing through wherever there is the least resistance. So you have no choice in this — being pulled by the pulls bringing geese up from the south and steelhead upriver and dandelions advancing like small soldiers.

There are lots of paths to follow on days like this, many ways to turn, but on this day (this is a spring day, and you do not fool anyone) you are drawn to the river and, newly freed of ice, how it crackles like blessings with the stories of life. On the trail between you and the river, however, lies the cemetery, a village of stones like the stones in the river — castles and warehouses, resting places and prisons.

You stop there, at the cemetery, the halfway point of your journey to the river — this is a well-known river up north here, and we'll call this the Pine Ridge Cemetery. You stop at Jackson's for lunch, for the sandwich in your pack, for the coffee, for the apple of Eden. That's too much, but this is spring, or almost spring, and this is Jackson's. Father. Fifty-three years open for business in the same location. Next to us is also Jackson. Mother. She joined her husband almost thirty years ago. She is quiet as an earthworm, though a long time ago she covered her farmer knees with dresses and bathed her earlobes with rosewater and went to big band dances. She could have.

There's Baby Girl Hower over there, 1948. Did the earth sing when it took her? There's Grandmother Hanson 1987. There's young George over there. And Bud. You miss Bud sometimes.

It'll happen to you, you think, on an autumn day as you're splitting wood, the axe poised high, and you're pulling for momentum. Or when you're raking leaves on a windy Saturday, and your heart's doing magical numbers in a duck blind. There'll come a tap on your shoulder and a dark whisper behind the echo of the wind, "It's time."

Whoa! It seems clear that you are to lay down your axe or your rake or your hammer, whatever. You are to take a last look at the leaves changing color, strain to hear farewell sobs of geese going south, inhale the music of the air thick with autumn. You are to climb into an appropriately prepared box, or slip into the fire and fly out past the moon, or curl up in some far-off farmyard flower forever and ever.

Soiled clouds hang in the sky. There is thunder.

"Sez who?" you say. "I need more time," you say. To strengthen your argument you say it again. "I need more time!"

On this dark and desolate day you explain the situation in which you find yourself, though you sound somewhat like a kid practicing the piano with one finger doing it. You say to the tapper, "I've got to sit again in the oak tree out back, the oak tree at the edge of the pasture, the oak tree too beautiful to lose. I've got to watch that doe and her fawns feed in the pasture. I've got to listen for the buck, just out of sight, snort in the startled stillness. Let my heart stop and my body stiffen at the suddenness of it, at the nearness of it, at the wonder of it.

"Just one more time I've got to ride a canoe loaded with decoys, loaded with distant skies, just the dog and me, into the crispness of an October morning. I've got to hear again the lifesaving sounds of mallards' wings. And while we're there, let's add a November morning and paint a bluebill in the picture. Let me hold my gun again.

"Hold on," you'll stall. "Under these extenuating circumstances, I must be allowed to drill another maple tree on a dazzling spring-winter tug-of-war day and listen to the drop, drip, drip of that splendid miracle. I need another go at the foxy trout in the silky Boxcar Pool."

In the wavering of an instant you consider dropping to the ground face down and holding your breath. You've heard it works sometimes with grizzly bears. "What harm can there be?" you say, suddenly feeling like an old man lying on a white bed not knowing who you are. "What harm can there be in another slow paddle down the river, in another campfire, in another majestic, soaring moonlit night?"

Your mercury rising, you get tough. "Give me another hour," you snarl, wishing you had a toothpick to dangle from the corner of your mouth. "Give me another hour high above the big lake. Give me an hour to lie on the cliff that juts out over the water. With my eyes closed and half dreaming, let me hear the lighthouse calling.

"I've got suckers in the smoker," you say, "and a leaky kitchen sink. I've got neighbors to thank for this and that. I need to tell my wife how I've loved her. I need to throw a stick for the dogs to fetch and a ball to the kid. As old as she is — can you believe she's thirteen already — I've got to hold her again, really tight."

You feel an uneasy creeping in your scalp. "I need to walk through ankle-deep leaves again, and cedar swamps, and smell the smells of bacon and eggs and fried potatoes cooking on a campfire. And fry bread.

"Who'll feed the chickadees next January? Who'll build the wood duck houses? What'll they do without me down at the Elkhorn Tavern and Wildlife Museum?

"Does the sun shine where I'm going? Does the wind sough through the pines? Do pheasants bring on the dawn and set the moon free? Can I bring my tent? Do they play pinochle? Is there crappie fishing? Will the heat be oppressive?"

The sun slides behind a cloud, and you feel a noticeable chill, and suddenly the Jacksons don't seem to be such good company. And you remember the couple of nice bucks you've gotten in your lifetime. You think back to a morning on the river years ago. And how you've canoed other rivers into and out of glorious days. And how you've seen Lake Superior perfectly calm and perfectly horrible. And how you've walked magnificent partridge woods and cornfields busting with birds. And how you've fished pretty trout streams and walleye waters. And how you've lain out nights when the stars were so bright you could play them like checkers, and how you've been actively involved with the northern lights. How you've had friends you couldn't have earned and a family better than you deserve. How once, when a greenhead came flashing by, you made one hell of a shot. How you've heard loons on moonlit lakes.

"Come on, Old Sport," you say, giving the guy with the scythe a little nudge in the ribs. "You win."

But right now, it's spring. Robins are coming home. Partridges are drumming. A frog newly roused from its muddy bed is coaxing a sweetheart from a swamp. A pair of teal go scudding across the sky.

There will be crabgrass and dandelions.

And time.

While my father and grandfather slept,

I silently climbed out of my bunk,

got into my clothes and walked out the

cabin door. A gray fog shrouded the lake.

Summer

The clouds seemed to hang on the treetops,

and the trees and the ground were

damp with dew. As I stared out at the lake,

I was startled by a wild, quavering cry

from a distant bay.

BOB RIEPENHOFF
From "A Northwoods Memory"

Don L. Johnson *began his outdoor writing career with the* Eau Claire Leader-Telegram *in 1951. He moved to* The Milwaukee Sentinel *in 1962, remaining there for twenty-two years before turning to freelancing full time. His byline has since appeared in many magazines, several books, and a wide range of other publications. Don's work has been honored by a long list of professional and conservation organizations. In 1991, he was inducted into the Media Hall of Fame by the Milwaukee Press Club. He and his wife, Lorraine, live in Menomonie, Wis., a location well suited to Don's desires to spend time on the streams with a fly rod, or in the woods and fields pursuing grouse.*

Reprinted by permission of the author.
This story first appeared in The Milwaukee Sentinel.

Reunion at the Brule

DON L. JOHNSON

Back upstream now for one more stop.
Two fishermen rest on the tailgate of
a dusty station wagon at the
Highway FF bridge. They have been on
the river for two days, long enough for
their chins to be stubbled and
for their eyes to look young again.

*I*t's just another river that glides beneath the Highway 2 bridge here at Brule. There are no spectacular views from the road, no racing rapids, no churning falls. Just a river. I have stayed away for a long time, so long that I had trouble recalling when I'd last felt the cool tug of those currents against my waders. Two years? Something like that. Neither am I sure what has brought me back. Not the fishing, for I have no rod, no boots, no time. What then?

The meetings that hurried me from Ashland to Bayfield have ended early, leaving me with unexpected hours before I have to catch a plane at Ironwood. Somehow then, the rented car has sought the route to remembered places and to reunions with old friends. If you follow at a distance, you will see only the river and me. Come closer, then.

There in the sweep of river below The Hogback, Mark Senn is standing, braced against the current, intent as a hungry heron as his line drifts; content as a sleepy seagull as he retrieves. There's an old cord stringer tied to his suspenders, and drifting at the other end is a rainbow as long as his forearm. He squints at the shimmering water for a clue as to where another big trout lies. Mark will always be there. They carved a trout on his tombstone when they buried him at Menomonie, but river stones mark his real resting place.

And the bootprints must still be there, beneath that new gravel on the red clay road. Here's where Roy Lyons, Jim Meyer and I made that long, weary walk after being caught by winter at season's end. Little floes of ice had been drifting by all day as we canoed down the Brule, casting with numb hands, wrestling with a cold, gray, stubborn river that refused to yield just one more fish for remembrance through the long winter.

Finally the ice began to pack up, shore to shore, and we could go no farther. We dragged the canoe into the woods and trudged the remaining miles to our intended takeout point. Night fell, the wind moaned, the snow swirled down. And we knew — the wind promised — that those same snowflakes would remain all winter. They would be waiting, in fact, when we returned to try again in spring.

Now there is Roy, in the stern of the canoe, pole braced to hold us above a likely looking eddy. How many times? I can't remember. But neither will I forget. You can no longer find Roy at The Lyons Den in Brule. He is gone. But I still see him when I look to the river.

Around the next bend now, there is a place where the river mutters around boulders. A really big man could use them as stepping stones. Wally Niemuth did it. I took a dunking when I tried. I plainly see Wally there, pensively watching the currents. A fish biologist who saw the Brule as much more than a fishery, he worked hard to keep it so. His spirit still lives here.

We are not alone. Four fishermen are waiting near the river mouth. They watch for trout to find breaches in sand barriers built by the river's current and Lake Superior's waves. They have caught no fish, but seem content to linger there, where waves sigh against the sand. The beach has been swept clean by a recent storm. There are only a few feathers, sculpted sticks and multicolored stones. And, surprisingly, ladybugs. Thousands, millions, of little red beetles jewel the shore.

Back upstream now for one more stop, one more look. Two fishermen rest on the tailgate of a dusty station wagon at the

Highway FF bridge. There the river turns and slides and sings. It is having a good time. The water is too low, too clear, the fishermen say. However, one has just lost a big trout, a steelhead that would go nine pounds, he vows. Both are from Illinois, middle-aged and more. They have been on the river for two days, long enough for their chins to be stubbled and for their eyes to look young again.

The men speak knowingly of the river. They have tried the Meadows without success. By evening they will try fly fishing the Big Lake stretch. We talk about trout and tackle and techniques.

"What's a trout fisherman doing here without a rod?" one finally wants to know.

"Just passing by on a quick trip," I explain. "I stopped for a visit with some friends."

And one of them was a river.

Bob Riepenhoff *is outdoor editor of* The Milwaukee Journal Sentinel. *His column, which appears each Sunday, chronicles his experiences as he travels across Wisconsin, hunting and fishing his way through the cycle of the seasons. Readers will find him wading a trout stream with a fly rod, casting musky plugs from a fishing boat, crouching low in a duck blind, or climbing high in a tree stand as he shares his experiences and the hopes, joys, laughter and heartaches that are all part of the outdoor life. Bob lives in Wauwatosa with his wife, Elise, sons Rob, John and Joe, and a golden retriever named Buck.*

A Northwoods Memory

BOB RIEPENHOFF

There was something magical
about this place. I could feel it in the
fresh smell of pines, in the uncountable
stars sparkling overhead, and in the
wisps of mist rising like ghosts from the
mirror-still surface of the lake.

One August night many years ago, a deer moved silently through a pine forest at dusk, skirting the edge of a small lake and pausing a safe distance from the light, the smell of woodsmoke, and the muffled voices from an isolated cabin. Inside were two men and a boy, talking, laughing and making plans.

"So, how does it feel to be Up North?" the old man asked the boy.

"It feels great," the boy replied. "Can we go fishing in the morning, Grandpa?"

"The weather's too nice," the old man said. "They won't be biting."

Seeing the disappointment on his son's face, the other man interrupted. "I'll take you out tomorrow." The boy's face brightened.

"Would anyone like to take a walk?" the grandfather asked. The father declined, opting to relax on the couch and stare into the flames of the fieldstone fireplace.

"I'll go, Grandpa," the boy said, springing up from his chair and reaching for the heavy wool shirt he used as a jacket.

That conversation took place more than thirty years ago, though it hardly seems possible that so much time has passed. But now, as I sort through a dusty old tackle box left forgotten in the corner of the attic, and uncover a small, red pocket knife, the scene comes back to me, strong and clear, from across the distance of time.

As I turn the knife over in my hand, open it, and run my finger along a tarnished steel blade, I recall my excitement at being alone for the first time with my father and grandfather on a fishing trip in Wisconsin's Northwoods. I can smell the smoke from the birch log fire as I watch the shadows dance on the dark logs of the cabin walls. I see my grandfather as he puts on his jacket and walks over to open the door, and I feel the chill of the night air as I follow him into the woods. If I close my eyes, I can almost hear his voice.

"The woods are beautiful just before dark," my grandfather said as we made our way along the trail that evening. "It's a lovely time to walk. All the wild creatures are stirring." Though the forest was all around us, I felt the strong presence of the lake. With each step we took, I could see patches of silver water shimmering through the trees and hear the voices of a thousand frogs singing to each other and to the approaching night. As we drew near to a towering evergreen tree, my grandfather paused for a moment.

"This is a white pine," he said, resting his hand on the wide trunk. "It's my favorite of all trees. They grow so straight and tall." His eyes slowly followed the tree all the way up to the sky and back to earth again, then looked straight into mine.

"You know that this is a working vacation for me, Bobby," he told me, a little uneasy. "I have a lot of writing to finish. So I won't have time to do all the things you might want me to do."

Then he reached into his pocket and pulled out a little red knife. "Here," he said. "I thought you might like this."

"Thanks, Grandpa," I said. I took a moment to open the blades and admire their lines and textures, then folded the knife down and carefully put it into my pocket. We walked on in silence as dusk gave way to darkness, then turned and headed back to the cabin. As we rounded a bend, there was a scurrying in the trees ahead, and I could just make out the white tail of a deer waving like a flag before it vanished into the woods.

"A lot of times, that's all you see of a deer," my grandfather said. "This is their world. Like all wild things, they are afraid of people. But every once in a while, if you are very quiet and still, you can get close."

When we reached the cabin, he said, "You'll be getting up early tomorrow. You'd better get some sleep."

"Can I walk down to the lake first?" I asked.

"OK. But then right to bed."

As I followed the narrow path that wound down to the lake, the chill of the crisp night air heightened my senses and made me feel strangely connected with everything around me. There was something magical about this place. I didn't really understand it, but the signs were all around me. I could feel it in the fresh smell of pines, in the uncountable stars sparkling overhead, and in the wisps of mist rising like ghosts from the mirror-still surface of the lake.

It was a change that had begun to settle on me that morning as my father's car left the pavement and turned onto the pine-canopied dirt road leading deep into the forest and into another world where everything was natural, wild, random and uncontrolled.

That night, my head was filled with visions of the creatures that roamed, wild and free, through the darkness that surrounded me. I thought of the deer my grandfather and I had seen, still out there somewhere in the woods, moving with stealth and grace like a phantom of the forest, its nose, ears and eyes ever alert. And I thought about fish, the big, toothy muskies, the bronze-backed walleyes and the full-bellied bass I had seen hanging in frozen poses on the walls of taverns and sporting good stores. Only now, I imagined a solitary, living predator, rising from the cool, deep water with a stroke of its powerful tail to cruise the night shallows.

I stood alone on the pier in the darkness that night, my mind hiking a meandering path through such thoughts, when a sudden, loud splash drew my eyes to the lake. For a long time, I watched the big circles expand on the surface in the moonlight, wondering what kind of fish would cause a commotion like that.

———————— ✐ ————————

I awoke at dawn the next day. While my father and grandfather slept, I silently climbed out of my bunk, got into my clothes, and walked out the cabin door and down to the lake. A gray fog shrouded the lake. The clouds seemed to hang on the treetops, and the trees and the ground were damp with dew. As I stared out at the lake, I was startled by a wild, quavering cry from a distant bay. I had not yet learned about loons, and I wondered for a moment if this eerie sound could be the voice of a spirit.

I got the rods and reels from my father's car, set them up, carried them down to the lake, and put them into the battered, weather-worn aluminum rowboat that, to me, was more precious than gold. I made a second trip for the tackle box, cushions and net, and a third for a cottage cheese container with holes poked in the lid and lots of night crawlers inside. Then I went back to the cabin to see if anyone was awake.

I opened the door to the smell of bacon and coffee and the sight of my grandfather at the stove, cooking over a black cast-iron skillet.

"Do you feel lucky this morning, Bobby?"

I had never seen my grandfather unshaven before. He looked so relaxed and comfortable with his whiskers and flannel shirt, and the stern, worried look he usually wore back in the city was absent from his face.

"Yes, Grandpa," I said, honored just to be with him in this special place. "I feel very lucky today."

———————— ✐ ————————

The bow of the rowboat cut a sharp wedge into the still surface of the lake as my father rowed, and I looked out into the fog. The soft sound of water against the oars, mixed with the weary squeaks of the rusty stays turning in the oarlocks, was magnified by the surrounding silence. As we drifted into a log-strewn bay, my father quietly tucked the oars inside the boat and got ready. Smoke from his cigarette lifted into the fog as he fixed lead sinkers to the lines and baited the hooks.

"Cast near the logs," he whispered. "Get as close as you can without getting hung up." I took great care, trying my best to cast near the fog-shrouded logs, but nothing happened. We continued rowing, drifting, casting, reeling, speaking seldom and in hushed tones when we did, as we made our way around the lake. Before long, the fog had burned off, and the once-gray water turned a deep blue-green. Now I could see all the details of the lake and woods.

It was a haunting vision. The unspoiled shoreline gave a sense of remoteness and tranquility that seemed to transcend time. I thought the lake must have looked the same a hundred or even a thousand years before. The peaks of countless pines formed a jagged green edge between forest and sky, a pattern repeated in mirror images on the water of the shady bays. Where the sunlight hit the shore, I could see among the ever-greens the narrow trunks of birches and aspens, their leaves quaking in the gentle breeze. There were quiet bays, scattered with tangled logs and clusters of lily pads, some with white blossoms adorning the water's surface. Trees toppled by wind and weather lay along the shoreline, broken trunks still rooted in the dark earth. The lake was peaceful and calm, yet alive with constant motion. It rippled with the movement of the oars, shimmered in the breeze and sparkled with the rays of sunlight.

As I studied the scenery, I continued to cast and reel. When I felt the strike, I wasn't really sure what it was. But my father knew. He saw my line jerk suddenly, then move toward a submerged tree, which would give a wise old largemouth bass a chance to wrap the line and break off. Experience told my father what to do. As I reeled, he grabbed the oars and, with a few quick strokes, headed us out to the deep water of mid-lake.

I held on with all my might as I reeled against the unseen force. But when the bass broke the surface in a head-shaking, line-stretching, splattering attempt to spit the hook, my heart really started to pound. The fish was so big it was frightening. It was wider than my father's boots and longer than the blades of the oars. In the instant of the jump I could see the black of its back, the white of its belly, the red of its gills, the fire in its eyes. And I felt the violent, thrashing power of its fury.

The bass fought on for a long time, but out in the middle of the lake there was nowhere for a big fish to hide. Finally, the bass grew tired, and I was able to bring it to the side of the boat and to the net waiting in my father's hands. We were both breathing deeply as we admired the fish I clutched in my hands.

"It's a real beauty," my father said proudly.

I just smiled.

Back at the cabin, my grandfather was deep in thought, working at his typewriter.

"How did you do?" he asked without looking up.

"We got only one, Grandpa," I said solemnly. Then, no longer able to hide my joy, I broke into a triumphant grin and swung a stringer holding the big bass out from behind my back. "Here it is! What do you think?"

His eyes grew wide, and he was moved to laugh his deep, wheezy laugh that always reminded me of the sound of a freight train trying to stop too quickly. "Congratulations, Bobby," he said, shaking his head. "I haven't seen one that big in quite some time." Then he got up from the table and left his work. "Go get your knife," he told me. "I'll show you how to clean that fish."

And so, that afternoon, with my grandfather's meticulous instruction, I learned the delicate art of making fillets on a flat piece of scrap wood behind the cabin in the shade of the pines. Later that evening, he got the cast-iron skillet out again, dusted the fillets in flour, fried them in oil, and served them with potatoes, corn and rye bread.

"Tonight we'll eat like kings because we have at least one fisherman in this family," Grandpa announced at the dinner table. My father laughed, and I beamed at the praise.

In the days that followed, there were more quiet mornings fishing on the lake, more afternoons hiking in the woods, more chilly nights with starlit skies and crackling fires, more precious time to spend with my father and grandfather.

And then it was time to leave. After we packed the car and cleaned the cabin, I made one more early morning trip down the path to the lake. I told my father I wanted to make sure we hadn't left anything in the boat, but the truth was I just wanted to say goodbye to the lake. As I stood alone on the pier looking out at the water and trees, taking it all in one last time, I felt real sadness. My heart longed for some way to capture the magic of this place, so I could always carry it with me. Reaching into my pocket, I felt the knife. I took it out and was holding it in my hand when I noticed something moving in the trees across the lake.

I stood motionless and watched. Three deer emerged from the woods and walked down to the lake to drink. They were just close enough so that I could see their faces. It was the first time I had seen deer without being seen first, and I felt thrilled and enchanted by their wild presence. As the deer lowered their heads to the water, I could see that the one in the middle had antlers. My heart was pounding.

Just then, the knife slipped from my hand and hit the pier with a terrible clatter that echoed and shattered the stillness. Across the lake, three heads lifted. I froze and held my breath, watching and waiting for the deer to turn and run. But they didn't. Instead, the buck fixed his gaze on me, and I stared back, spellbound. As our eyes locked, an eternity passed. Then all three deer lowered their heads to finish drinking before, one by one, they slowly turned and their flag-tails fluttered and vanished into the forest.

It seems strange now, after so many years have passed, that an old, forgotten pocket knife has become the the talisman I longed for so deeply on that sad morning when I had to leave the place that had captured my heart. As a boy, I never dreamed the knife would take on such sacred power. But time has transformed my childhood gift. Now, as I pick it up and hold it in my hand, its power is unleashed, mysterious wheels are set in motion, and the memories come flooding back.

Before long, I am back there in the woods of northern Wisconsin, staring into the glowing warmth of a cabin fireplace, gliding silently in a boat through the fog, or standing on a pier in the moonlight watching circles on the water grow so big that they disappear. And, just for an instant, I see the sudden splash of a big bass exploding from the depths of my memory, or hear the voice of my grandfather calling to me from across the years, or maybe glimpse eternity in the eyes of a deer.

That's when I feel the magic of the woods once again.

Mel Ellis *(1912-84) is best remembered for his nature writing, but he was also among the best hunting and fishing writers of his time. He was outdoor editor of* The Milwaukee Journal *for 15 years and an associate editor of* Field & Stream *for 12 years. During the 1950s and 1960s, his byline appeared frequently in major outdoor publications. Ellis ultimately turned away from the hook-and-bullet scene to concentrate on nature writing. He published 18 books, and two of them,* Wild Goose, Brother Goose *and* Flight of the White Wolf, *became Disney TV movies. His following among Wisconsin readers has been restored by the release of two books of his nature writing,* Notes From Little Lakes *(1996) and* The Land, Always the Land *(1997), both published by The Cabin Bookshelf, Waukesha, Wis. The accompanying story, a memoir, was one of very few fishing stories Ellis wrote after the 1960s.*

Reprinted by permission of the Larry Sternig/Jack Byrne Literary Agency. This story first appeared in Fishing Wisconsin *magazine in 1980.*

Those Special Trout

MEL ELLIS

A split second after the streamer hit
the water, I saw a flash of color.
A fish darted out from beneath the bank
and rolled beneath the streamer without
making contact. An accident, I told myself.
Perhaps the last fish in the creek.

As Izaak Walton is my witness, this is a true story.

It was the year after World War II. After nearly five years of being 16033084, I was trying to be me again, and to travel back down through the years, to the time when fishing had been my safety valve, a guaranteed way of keeping my perspective, of moving along on the mainstream of life on a reasonably even keel.

But it wasn't working. I went to Dodge County to the Rock River of my boyhood, and I knew, even as the boat slid smoothly out into the lazy current, that I shouldn't have come, that the magic was gone. Perhaps it was my age, and it was too late to recapture the days of my youth. Perhaps it was the rigors of war and, as some were saying, I was really flak-happy. Or, perhaps it was the river itself.

The Rock presented a dismal picture. Where once there had been hundreds, now there were but a few white-billed coots, heads bobbing at their every querulous inquiry. Rarely did ducks lift to angle on a curve of the wind, to fly to some safer place. Where there had been floating green lawns of lily and spatterdock pads, small gardens of duck potato, tangles of coontail, now brown cattails had put up impenetrable barriers. There was scum at the waterline on shoreside rocks. There was even an odor, and the once-coppery water had a gray cast, and it did not sparkle in the sun.

I caught a northern of the size we called hammer handles and headed for shore. I knew if I were to recapture the magic, put to rest the turbulent years, it was not going to happen on the Rock. Back in my room near Milwaukee's 27th Street and Wisconsin Avenue, I wallowed in self-pity for several weeks, then decided to give fishing one more try. Cars were still at a premium, but I had an old Model A Ford I had saved from the junkyard, and I decided to try the sand country trout streams. When my father had fished them, we took a train to Oshkosh and then, hiring a rig, trotted horses west to Waushara County. I had tented there as a boy, fished more than a score of streams all within a twenty-mile radius of one another, and successfully resisted growing up by spending weeks immersing myself in an orgy of fishing.

On nearing the farm I had always used as a base camp, I was surprised to see, on crossing the creek, that the waters had not lost their shine and that the bank grasses were not trampled but stood high and tawny with enough wildflowers topping out to make them scintillate. I walked into Marvin Semrow's barn shortly after sunrise. He was milking. After talking about many things, I asked, "How's the fishing?"

"Mel, there are no fish. The state hasn't stocked the stream in years. Since before the war. The creek's empty."

"I don't believe it," I said.

"Well, go see for yourself."

My enthusiasm gone, I crossed a pasture, crawled beneath a fence, and maneuvered my way through bogs. The blackbirds were still in residence and protested my trespass. There was a bobolink singing on high, and meadowlarks were bright as butter on fence posts. When I came to the creek, I parted the bank grasses, and there it ran, swift and clear. I could even feel an updraft of cool air.

I rigged up a seven-and-a-half-foot fly rod, dressed my line, and tied on a leader, which tapered down to a tippet testing a pound. Tying on a dry fly — I even remember that it was a

Royal Coachman — I started fishing upstream. An hour, and not a rise. I tried fishing a Muskrat's Regret wet. Still nothing. Then, almost panicking, I fished nymphs, and before I knew it, the sun had passed the zenith, and I had not seen a single fish dimple the surface. Marv had been right. There were no fish. I walked back up the slope to the farm home. Marv was in the shade of a box elder letting his lunch settle.

Before I could say anything, he said, "Didn't I tell you?"

What could I say? The stream was in excellent condition. It had always been noted for its ability to produce its own trout — mostly browns, plus a few brooks — and it had always been heavily stocked. I said nothing for a while, and then asked, "You sure that no one has been fishing the creek?"

"Not more than a dozen guys in the last four years. Ever since the war. What with rationing ... "

"I know," I interrupted. "But a stream like that can't ever be really fished out, not down to the last trout."

Marv shook his head. "You may be right, but all I know is that I haven't seen a single trout. Not even while spearing suckers in spring." I started back down the slope. "You going to try again?" Marv called out after me.

"Yeah," I said. "I'm going to give it one more whirl."

It seemed important that I try. I sensed I had arrived at a very crucial time in my life. I had but two choices. I could resume living with my old vigor to recapture a career, a home, a life that the war had taken. Or I could gradually drift toward a lonely, one-bulb room with a bed, a chair and a table with a bottle of wine on it.

I tried every fly in my folder, plus a few atrocities from my hatband. I kicked a rotting stump and offered the fish a grub. I dug with the toe of my boot and soaked a worm. Then I sat on the bank exhausted, and as I sat, the sweat dried on my face, and my cheeks cooled. A wind whipped up, and I began to shiver beneath my sweat-soaked shirt. I looked up. Black clouds had ganged up in the west and were scudding in my direction. I was a quarter-mile from the farm. Might as well quit, head for the barn before the rain came.

My old fishing hat was in my hands. How many times and in how many places had I worn it? I turned it slowly in my hands, then stopped when an ancient and ragged Mickey Finn came into focus. How many fish? I could even remember some of the larger ones the streamer had fooled. Why not? Just once, for a little while, and for times gone.

The wind picked up. I crowded the edge of the stream, but stayed out of the water. The wind was pushing, and I had to make up for the lack of backbone in the little rod by slamming on my forward cast. A split second after the streamer hit the water, I saw a flash of color. A fish darted out from beneath the bank and rolled beneath the streamer without making contact. Again, and he was hooked.

An accident, I thought. Perhaps the last fish in the creek. I broke the brown's neck and almost lovingly cuddled its thirteen inches among the ferns in my creel. Wiping my hands on my pants, I moved a dozen feet and cast downstream. I brought the streamer darting back: three feet, six feet, nine … a bright streak. The line stopped. The rod bent. A ten-incher.

Bank grasses were galloping. There was lightning and thunder, but no rain. Another fish, a nine-inch brookie. Move, cast. Move, cast. Always downstream. Four fish. Seven. Nine. On other days I would have stopped with four. But this was special, a very special day. And then, when I had nine, I cast again, lost my hold on the line, and the Mickey Finn tumbled on slack to disappear in a deep hole at a bend.

When I regained control of the line, I met with resistance. It took me a long time to lead the fish upstream to where I could slide it into an inlet and beach it. It was a brown. It would weigh four pounds.

Night had darkened the farmyard by the time I slid the barn door open. I stepped in just as rain began to hammer on the tin roof. Marv was milking by lantern light. When he saw the big brown trout dangling from a line tied to my belt, I thought he was going to faint. Then when I opened the creel and showed him the other nine, I had to put out a hand to keep him from teetering off the milking stool.

I left without giving Marv a single fish. These were mine because they probably were the most important fish I had ever caught or would ever catch. I was going to eat them all, one every morning for breakfast. And whenever I felt fearful that I had left behind, perhaps on some foreign soil, that love of life that is so necessary to pick up the pieces and start over again, I would remember that beautiful little creek and the trout that weren't there.

Sharon Hart Addy *grew up playing on the Lake Michigan beach in the park near her Oak Creek home, wading in the waves, and fishing with her dad. She never moved away for long, just for a few years when she was single and teaching. She is best known in writing circles for her children's books,* A Visit with Great Grandma *and a guide to Milwaukee County titled* Kidding Around Milwaukee. *Sharon has also sold articles and stories to magazines for adults and children. Now that her kids are on their own, she has time to indulge her interests in bird watching and wildflowers. During the summer, she follows her husband around a wooded archery range, guidebooks and camera in hand.*

The Breakwater

SHARON HART ADDY

*Pop didn't seem to notice the
change in temperature, or even that it was
a wind and not a breeze. Then the shadow
of the harbor light darkened, and the
water turned gray. Behind us, to the south,
thick clouds boiled across the skyline
as far as we could see.*

Seagulls soared, white against a clear blue sky, their cries piercing the air, mingling with the slap of waves against the breakwater. The damp morning breeze wrapped around my bare arms and legs and brought goose bumps.

I didn't regret wearing shorts and a sleeveless blouse, even though Pop had looked skeptically at my stick-like eleven-year-old legs when we started off on our fishing adventure.

Fishing the breakwater scared me, but I had agreed to go after an encounter Pop and I had with my uncle. A few weeks before, we'd gone to see if the fish were biting in the creek where it ran through Grant Park. My uncle was standing on the bank, alone.

"I'm going fishing with my buddy on Memorial Day," my uncle announced, as if giving an excuse for fishing by himself. The rivalry between my dad and my uncle was more than casual.

My dad rose to the bait. "I'm taking my fishing buddy, too," he answered.

"Oh?" Disbelief dripped from my uncle's words. "Who's that?"

Dad slipped his arm around me. "My son here."

I swelled with pride. To be called my father's son was greater praise and acceptance than I'd ever received before.

My uncle wiped his hand across his mouth and chin. He didn't chuckle, but from the expression on his face he might have. "Well then," he replied, "we'll be looking for you."

As Memorial Day grew closer, I thought more and more about the afternoon the summer before when the whole family fished off the breakwater. We sat on the top, our legs resting against the slanted sides, while waves bobbed along the flat area several feet lower. We were near the end, where the breakwater squared off to hold the tall iron supports of the harbor light. The fish weren't biting.

It would have been nice to walk around under the light where there was enough room to move freely, but getting there meant walking along the narrow top. Mooring posts spaced along it squatted like huge black mushrooms, their round caps almost as wide as the breakwater's top. We had stepped around them to get to where we were sitting, so I knew there was room to get past them, but not enough as far as I was concerned. I was sure that while maneuvering around one, I would lose my balance and land in the lake. Even sitting still on the top of the breakwater, legs pressed against the slanted side, eyes on the flat lower ledge, I felt pulled toward the water, destined to fall in and drown.

That day I managed to conquer my fear and walk off the breakwater confidently. As I thought of walking it again, my fear returned and multiplied. But I couldn't back out. Pop had told my uncle I'd be there. I was his fishing buddy, his son.

As Pop took the fishing gear from the car, I stared at the breakwater stretching toward the horizon. I knew that all the way out to the end, where he liked to fish, I'd be watching my footing, making sure I wasn't stepping off the edge or bumping into a mooring post. But first, just far enough from shore so that the lake was deeper than I was tall, we would come to the damaged stretch where the smooth concrete top was gone and the surface was a rounded, pebbly mound.

Pop saw me hesitate as he started down the breakwater with the minnow bucket and tackle box. "There's nothing to be afraid of," he said. "It's like walking a sidewalk." His words were no comfort. I followed him, the knot in my stomach matched only by the lump in my throat. I could see myself tripping, rolling down the slanted side, crossing the flat area at the bottom, and splashing into the lake, never to be seen again.

I watched my feet as I walked. Pop watched for my uncle. It was early in the day. There weren't many people fishing, but sometimes Pop would stop to ask someone, "Are they biting?"

Absorbed in my fear, I would walk on, surprised to find myself alone. Pop was two or three mooring posts back, gabbing with strangers. I listened as I waited.

Pop was saying, "… beautiful day for it. We drove down from Milwaukee. My brother and his buddy are along here somewhere. Usually I fish with my wife, but she's working today. She's a waitress at this little restaurant and … ."

I stopped listening and studied the clear sky. The weather report had predicted a perfect spring day: sunshine with a light breeze and temperatures promising warmth.

Eventually, Pop noticed me waiting. "You could have gone ahead," he told me as we walked together.

I said, "That's okay." I didn't want to remind him I was afraid.

We found my uncle and his friend on the concrete platform under the light at the end of the breakwater. I was glad to reach them. We were out on the lake as far as we could go on foot, and I knew the water was many times deeper than I was tall, but the area was big enough to make me feel safe.

While Pop made up the lines, I went around and under the rust-colored supports that held the light. After that long distance of tightrope walking, it felt good to move freely.

My uncle and his buddy fished with their legs hanging over the breakwater's edge. The sides here went straight down until they disappeared in the restless, beckoning water. When Pop had my line ready, I took it and sat back, holding it high enough so it wouldn't touch the breakwater's edge as it slid into the water. We fished facing north, the Milwaukee skyline a hazy silhouette under a light blue sky. The lake gleamed with moving patches of blue, green and silver. As morning passed, the quiet surface became a place of peaks and troughs.

Although the water's surface was eight to ten feet below us, my uncle began to complain that his shoes were getting wet. "The lake's getting rough," he said to Pop. "We're going." I wanted to go with them, but I didn't say anything. After all, Pop had called me his son. Would a son complain?

"It's not that bad," Pop answered. "We'll stay awhile."

Not long after they left, the wind grew cold. I shivered in my shorts and sleeveless blouse. Pop didn't seem to notice the change in temperature, or even that it was a wind and not a breeze. Then the shadow of the harbor light darkened and the water turned gray. He looked up and around. Overhead, black clouds rolled north. Behind us, to the south, thick clouds boiled across the skyline as far as we could see.

"Pack up!" Pop yelled.

The wind grew stronger with each second, blowing my hair into my eyes, slamming the lid on the tackle box, sending our lunch bag skittering over the edge, ripping the words from our mouths so we had to shout to each other. For one scary moment, Pop stood as if debating: Should we run for shore, or wait out the storm where we were? I wanted desperately to run, to move, to unleash the terror I felt.

Pop looked at me, shivering with cold and fear, then yelled, "Let's go!"

Head down, I ran. Waves shattered against the breakwater. Wind-driven spray spattered the top. I was suddenly aware that my tennis shoes were old, the soles worn smooth. Would they grip when the concrete was completely wet? I wanted to run faster, but I couldn't. I had to struggle past mooring posts and around slow-moving fishermen whose poles and buckets swung with the wind.

I saw grownups, some with children, huddled on the lower ledge of the north side of the breakwater, protected from the whipping wind. As waves swelled high enough to wash the ledge, more people scrambled to the top and ran for shore. More people, howling wind, slippery concrete. There was no running now. Bent over, I battled the wind. Each time I threw a leg forward the wind caught it and tried to blow it out from under me. I fought to keep my balance, to keep moving.

I felt someone push alongside me, between me and the wind. Something hit my back and knocked me flat. I heard a bucket rattle down the slanted side of the breakwater. Something soft, warm, and heavy landed partly on me.

"Pop!"

"We'll wait here until the wind lets up."

We lay there, his arm half-circling a mooring post while the wind screamed and the wave spray pelted us. We were there just long enough for me to catch my breath when he said, "Let's go."

Bent double, we ran for safety. Pop kept his arm around me and held me tight. His body blocked the wind, but as I threw my legs out to run, the wind pushed them aside like pickup sticks. When the wind eased up a bit, I dared to look ahead, to judge the distance to safety, but mostly I saw my feet pounding concrete. Then, when we were almost at shore, we came to the spot where the flat surface was broken away. Pop hesitated. The mound was lower than the rest of the breakwater. Powerful waves hammered it, jolting pebbles from the crumbling surface. The pebbles rolled into the angry lake as the waves drained away, then were thrown up again with the next assault.

Pop and I weren't the only ones watching waves surge over the mound. Several groups huddled to the side as if they had given up hope of crossing. Splintering waves battered us with icy drops as Pop judged the risk.

A man crouched near us with his son, hollered against the roaring wind and bashing waves, "Don't do it!"

Pop looked at me. My yearning for solid ground was stronger than my fear. I nodded. He tightened his grip. We jumped down onto the mound and leaped across it in long strides, my feet barely touching the surface. We reached the end of the mound, and his hold stayed tight as we jumped up to the firm, flat, undamaged surface.

Rain came, first in huge drops that stung like hail, then in a downpour. Sand replaced waves alongside the breakwater. The parking lot was just ahead. Pop let go. Heavy raindrops beat us as we dashed for the car and fought the wind to open the doors. Once inside we laughed with joy, relief, hysteria. We'd made it.

Pop started the engine and turned the heater on high. Rain smeared across the windows. Wind rocked the car. Through swipes of the windshield wipers, we caught glimpses of others who dared to run the mound racing to their cars. We waited until the worst of the storm played itself out, then drove to the restaurant where my mother was working.

By the time we arrived I had stopped shivering, but Pop and I were still cold and soaked from the rain. We sat at the counter. Mom came over right away.

"Thank God you're safe. We kept hearing about the storm on the radio … ." She reached across the counter to squeeze our hands. "Did you make it off the lake in time?"

Pop didn't answer directly. "We could both use a cup of coffee."

I smiled. Coffee. Not hot chocolate, not hot tea. Coffee. The grown-up's drink. I'd had it at home, but I'd never been allowed to drink it in public. While I sipped the hot brew Mom listened as Pop told about our escape. He told of the black clouds, the crashing waves, the rush of people running for shore. He told how he had to push his way through to catch up with me, how he knocked me down so I wouldn't be blown into the lake, and how I gave the nod to run the crumbling mound.

Mom interrupted to tell us the radio reported winds of sixty miles an hour. Trees and buildings had been blown over, and a lot of places were without power. Eventually we'd said all there was to say about the storm. The conversation wound down to the equipment we had lost and the customers Mom had served that morning.

At the time, the Memorial Day fishing trip didn't seem to make any difference in our lives, but now, as I look back, I know it did. I should have recognized the change the next time my father and I encountered my uncle fishing at the creek.

"My buddy and I are fishing the breakwater Saturday," my uncle said.

"I've been thinking about it," Pop volunteered.

My uncle's grin was cocky. "By yourself?"

Pop slipped his arm around my shoulders. "I thought

maybe my son here ... ." His words faded as he looked at me. There was an odd silence and a seriousness in his manner that froze the moment in my memory. My uncle moved or made a sound or something that brought back my awareness of him, the creek, and the original question.

My father cleared his throat. "Maybe my daughter will go with me."

"Sure," I answered, "I'll go fishing with you ... " I was going to call him Pop, the way I always did, but the word wouldn't come out. It seemed too breezy, too flip, not conveying the respect he deserved. I called him Dad.

Tom Joseph *has written stories for literary and mainstream magazines, and an excerpt from his novel,* Two Points, *appears in* Transactions, *a publication of the Wisconsin Academy of Sciences, Arts and Letters. A writer and municipal judge, Tom lives with his wife and three daughters in Manitowish Waters, Wis., where he cross-country skis, cooks Thai, canoes, and volunteers at the North Lakeland Discovery Center, a nonprofit outdoor education facility. He also backpacks a float tube into remote Northwoods lakes to fly fish, watch nature, and dream up stories.*

Laughing Eyes

TOM JOSEPH

I shinnied up a skinny black spruce.
Sure enough, a few hundred yards
dead ahead was the lake. I thought how
pumped Dad and Ernie must have been.
It's one thing to know by the map that
a lake is there, entirely another to find it
after bushwhacking through swampy hell.

Ernie the bagger at the I.G.A. and my Dad were fishing buddies. Ma always said what made them friends was they had the same eyes, which was a strange observation, since Ernie's were as green as Dad's were blue. Laughing eyes, she called them, eyes that never quite grew up. But Dad was gone four years now, and Ernie's eyes had lost their zip. You could hear it in his voice, too. Sure, he'd talk fishing, but it was polite talk, hear they're doing real good on the Flowage with leadheads and leeches kind of stuff.

I figured he'd hung it up for good when he said he was thinking about giving his notice, because fishing was the whole reason Ernie bagged groceries. As a young man he'd had a bait store, but he said guys knew to keep their guard up there, so he never picked up any decent info. He tried bartending with the same result. Customers' lips were loose enough. Problem was there was nobody home between the ears. But at the I.G.A. Ernie'd catch guys unawares. It was a form of hypnosis, really. He'd mesmerize them with his bagging skills, tossing groceries up like a juggler and directing them softly into their bags, all the while making fishing small talk. By the time Ernie finished packing, giving the bags his trademark quarter-turn to demonstrate their stability, he'd invariably have another rock bar or weed bed to try.

That was the Ernie of old, though. Now I could barely stand to watch him load me up. No juggling, no quarter turn. He mechanically packed my groceries and plunked the bags into my cart. I asked him, out of habit, if he wanted to go fishing. Not bothering to wait for his polite "Some other day," I pushed the cart toward the door. Instead, Ernie called out, "Pick me up at 4:30."

I articulated something to the effect of "Hnngh?"

"Bring a boat, mud minnows, and tennies," Ernie said.

I nodded.

"Make that a light boat," Ernie added. "You're gonna be dragging it a long way."

If there was a way to fish the lakes of northern Wisconsin, Dad and Ernie had tried it. They jigged for walleyes, cast for muskies, trolled for lake trout. They weren't even above dunking stumps for panfish. But Ernie's instructions could have only one meaning. We were going bass fishing. My memory clicked to the smell of swamp. A couple of evenings a summer, a dank, earthy odor would rouse me from my room and carry me to the kitchen, where I'd come upon the two of them grinning and holding a stringer of fat largemouth bass. Swamp was splattered on their glasses and fishing jackets, caked the length of their khakis. Brown muck oozed from their sneakers onto the towels Ma had laid out. Then, sipping bourbon from shot glasses, Dad and Ernie would tell us the evening's tale.

Oh, there were some good ones. One time they'd managed to bury Dad's truck to the frame in some soft ground and had to walk and hitch back to town to get a tow truck, and he got stuck too, so they called a bigger tow truck and darned if he didn't do the same, even though they warned the guy not to back down so far, so finally they hot-wired some logger's cat and pulled the whole mess, big wrecker, little wrecker, Dad's truck and trailer out like some backwoods circus train. Or maybe the tale would be more modest, about how they'd watched an otter swim right up to the boat and stick his neck way out, all curiosity, then cut a vee through the glass-calm lake and settle on the far shore to munch his minnow dinner.

"Sounded just like celery stalks," Ernie might say, and the two of them would nod. When they talked like this there'd be something extra in their voices. A certain reverence. Sometime during the telling, one of us would always demand to know what lake they were fishing. The answer was always the same. Lard Lake.

Lard Lake. You know. Near Banana Creek. Haven't been there? Well, do you know where Ella's Inlet is? No? About that far from her outlet.

Har har. Dad and Ernie would slap their muddy thighs, drip some more muck on the towels, and pour another bourbon. And of course, I'd scour the topo maps Dad had taped to the dining room wall. There wasn't any Lard Lake. Not anywhere. Though Dad took us bass fishing, we never went to that lake. Fisherman's code, he said. Ernie had shared it in the strictest confidence. Dad wasn't about to break that, not even with his own kids. Seems Ernie had finagled the lake's whereabouts from Opal Kerner, who'd beat it out of her husband, Frank, one night when he showed up reeking and way late for a family dinner. Ernie'd never fished the lake till Frank passed away. Now, said Dad, it was Ernie's to do with as he saw fit.

Nevertheless, Dad apparently wanted to horn in on Lard Lake permanently, because when he died, we found a handwritten attachment to his will reading, "Being of sound mind and body, well sound mind anyway, if my body was in decent shape I wouldn't be wasting my time writing this note, I hereby declare that I'd like my body cremated and the ashes spread in Lard Lake. Ask Ernie, he knows where it is."

We did ask Ernie, but by then it was pointless, since Ma had already announced that Dad's ashes weren't going anywhere, they were going to stay home by the fireplace to make up for all those nights he'd been tramping around in the likes of Lard Lake.

At the funeral we showed Ernie the note and told him Ma's decision. All he said was, "Guess she's right, boys." Ernie looked so sad and alone. We asked him if he wanted something of Dad's, his good rod or his tackle box or something.

"His fishing jacket, if it's not too much trouble," Ernie answered. It was a pink and black plaid affair, faded and stained, with a hole in the right pocket that Dad was always forgetting about, so his keys and loose change were constantly falling out. That jacket was Dad's pride and joy. We told Ernie we'd be honored.

Come to think of it, I hadn't seen that jacket since. I wondered if Ernie would be wearing it tonight. I stuffed my knapsack with weedless hooks, yellow twister tails, splitshot, needle nose pliers, stringer. What else did they carry on their Lard Lake trips? Oh yeah — Dad's yellow waterproof camera case, which doubled as a traveling minnow bucket. I threw the duck boat and oars in the truck and made for the store. Ernie came out, already in his khakis. He didn't have the fishing jacket on, but he was wearing a long-sleeved shirt, even though it was a warm day.

"You know what day it is?" he asked. Of course I did. Four years to the day. Would I ever forget how pitifully clean Dad looked in that hospital bed?

"Do I need to be blindfolded?" I asked.

"Wouldn't do wonders for your driving, now would it?" Ernie pointed me down the gravel road past the old fire tower. A good twenty-five miles of nothing but the flat expanse of a vast northern cedar swamp lay ahead. From the road there wasn't much to see other than scrubby tamaracks and tufts of marsh grass. We drove a ways and a half to where a finger of high ground stuck into the swamp.

"Pull over," Ernie said.

Leaving his stuff behind, Ernie headed into the woods. He returned shortly with a handful of plump blueberries. "Tradition," he said, dropping half into my hand. "You'll need the energy."

We donned our knapsacks, and Ernie led the way. I had little trouble pulling the light boat through the needly carpet under the tall pines. Then we reached the end of the high ground.

"No picnic from here," Ernie said. "It's another mile."

He was right. My first step took me knee-deep in a soft muck that tried to suck the sneaker off my foot.

"Think light," Ernie said. I watched him hop from tuft to tuft ahead of me, barely getting his feet wet. I couldn't exactly imitate him; I had the boat. So I slogged on through the primal goo. After about fifty struggling paces I stopped, lungs burning, sweat beading under my fishing hat and pushing down my temples. As I waited to catch my breath, my nostrils flared in remembrance. No doubt about it. It was the smell of late-night Dad and Ernie.

Ernie regarded me with, well, laughing eyes. "Here, I'll take it." There being a mile minus fifty feet of swamp left, I didn't protest. It didn't surprise me when he pulled it three times the distance I had. He kept moving after letting go of the boat, and gave a one-word explanation.

"Bugs."

Right again. My bare arms were positively furry with mosquitoes and deer flies. No wonder Ernie had worn a long-sleeved shirt. I tried to brush them off, but the deer flies hung on like pit bulls. Well, never mind. I grabbed the boat and noticed I made much better progress now that I was revved up to fleeing speed. So it went for the next forty-five minutes. The boggy ground gave way to alder thicket, which scratched and clawed at us. Then it got wet again as we followed the winding course of a stagnant creek littered with deadfall. By this time, Ernie was as sweaty and bit-up as I was, but every time I looked at him I saw that boyish dancing in his bright green eyes.

Ernie told me to sniff the air, and I got the sweet whiff of cedar. We were in the heart of the swamp. My own heart beat hard with exertion and excitement.

"Don't really need to, but why don't you climb a tree?" he said. "That's how your Dad and I first laid eyes on the lake."

I shinnied up a skinny black spruce. Sure enough, a few hundred yards dead ahead was the lake. I thought how pumped Dad and Ernie must have been. It's one thing to know by the map that a lake is there, entirely another to find it after bushwhacking through swampy hell. As we staggered to the lake, I asked Ernie why he and Dad didn't just leave a boat there. He told me it didn't matter how far the lake was, or how hard to get into, or how well you hid the boat, if you left one, somebody'd find it. Lard Lake was the only lake that he was pretty sure didn't get fished, not by anyone.

When we finally reached the shore, I looked the lake over. It was, without doubt, a bass fisherman's dream. The boggy shore was cluttered with logs, and the lake was ringed by lily pads, the smaller kind that indicate deeper water. There would be a good drop-off at the outside edge. That's where the big ones should be this time of year.

"Let's go fishing," I said.

"Hold on there, partner. We got plenty of time. I, for one, could use a little swim. Another tradition."

Then Ernie stripped and dove into the lily pads. Magical energy propelled his old man's body. I followed. The mineral-dark water was cool and incredibly soothing. We redressed, loaded the boat, and shoved off. Ernie told me to put fresh water in the camera case.

"Should I bait up? " I asked.

"No, there's something I need to show you," Ernie said. He rowed toward a bay with a large beaver house and pointed toward an overhanging tamarack that had a rag or something tied onto it. As we got closer, I recognized the pink and black pattern. Though tattered and more faded than ever, it was unmistakably Dad's fishing jacket.

"I've been coming here once a year," Ernie said. "Zipped it up the first year and walked back just to see it and take a swim the last two. Haven't fished."

Ernie's face looked old again, but he smiled a little as he said, "Your Ma should have his ashes, but I figured Lard ought to have his jacket." He turned away from me, and we both stared at that raggedy coat for a long time. I felt a jambalaya of sadness, humility and solace.

Ernie maneuvered the boat to shore, reached out and part-ed the moss to reveal a pitcher plant. "Venus's-flytrap of the North," he said. "They're getting to be as rare as good bass lakes, but you'll find plenty growing in the bog here. Old Frank and your Dad and I have all been lucky to know this place. It's special. Now it's your turn." He paused. "We'll fish around the lake and end up here."

I tied on my snap swivel, put on a splitshot, weedless and tail, and hooked a big mud minnow through the lips. Tossing it to shore, I dragged it over a log and slowly through the lilies.

As it reached the outer edge of the lily pads I let it drop. A few seconds later my line went taut with that nice solid feel of a good bass. I gave him slack so he wouldn't feel the hook and waited fifteen seconds or so, then snapped my wrist. My rod bent, and the line peeled out toward the lilies, but I held the rod high and was able to work the fish back. He gave me a couple of jumps and runs, but I knew I had him. Ernie netted him, a nice eighteen-incher, probably two-and-a-half pounds.

"Want to keep him?" Ernie asked. I thought of those big stringers he and Dad always brought back and tried to visualize myself at the other end from Ernie. It didn't feel right.

"Nah," I said. "I'd hate to have Dad's jacket hanging over a lake with no fish in it." For the next hour Ernie rowed, and I caught fish steadily, just about all in the sixteen- to twenty-inch range. For the Northwoods, those are dandies.

There wasn't much sunlight left. By now we'd reached the bay with the jacket. Ernie directed me to cast in front of the beaver lodge. I did, and in the deep water in front of the house I had a strike. It wasn't like the others. Hit light, held it a few seconds, then dropped it. I reeled in. No minnow. I rebaited and cast again with the same result. Next time I tried to hook quick, but I must have ripped the minnow out of his mouth, because it came out skinned clean. I knew it had to be a bass of some size; a small one won't skin the minnow. I cast it back out. Chomp. I counted one-one thousand, two, and struck, then reeled in the slack line on which nothing remained but mud minnow lips. I reached in the camera case. Great. Last minnow.

"Now what?" I asked Ernie.

"Try this and strike quick," Ernie said. He produced an old Stanley Weedless. I hadn't seen one for years. On its stem was a silver spinner mounted in front of a long-shanked hook. A couple of thin wires formed the primitive weedless. I remembered Dad teaching me to stick the hook down the minnow's mouth and out his gills, then twist it around and bury it in the minnow's back. Rigged like that, you didn't wait until the fish swallowed, you struck like Ernie said. I cast the final minnow, hoping the bass was pig enough to strike once more.

What largemouth isn't? I felt the tug, set the hook hard and wham! he was on. The fish ran wildly away from the beaver house, and I thought I was in luck, until I realized he was charging straight for the boat.

"Row out!" I yelled to Ernie as I reeled like mad, but the old-timer already was. Ernie pulled hard to one side, and I was able to work the line around the bow as the fish whizzed by. Then he jumped, one of those tail-dancing, head-shaking, slow-motion leaps. In that frozen instant, I saw this was no eighteen-incher. He was a swamp-injected monster of a bass, his back as broad as a two-by-four, his head enormous, the smooth arc of his open gills nearly cutting him in two. The dark stripe extending from gills to tail wasn't solid, rather a series of dabs from a brush dipped in a bucket of half-green, half-black paint. Under the Charleston green stripe, the white belly bulged with a lot more than the mud minnows I'd fed him. The sag of old age, I wondered? The tail, in comparison, looked puny. It couldn't possibly propel him out of the water, which, of course, it just had.

All this I saw in the split second of that first jump. And one thing more. There was something strange about him, something … unfishly. He landed, dove and swam back toward shore, moving more leisurely now, almost like he was out for his evening constitutional. He headed in the general direction of the beaver lodge, underneath which I knew, and I knew he knew, was a tangle of submerged brush. If he made it there I could kiss him goodbye. I tightened my drag as much as I dared, but my six-pound test was no match for him. My line snapped tight in the lilies. This fish knew all the moves. He had me.

Then, for some reason, he stopped. Like he decided wrapping the line around a log would be too easy. Like he was challenging me to give him my best shot. So be it. Ernie picked his way ever so carefully through the lilies, and I snaked the line between them, trying to keep tension on, until once again my rod pointed at the beaver house. Ernie slowly rowed me and the strangely compliant fish back to unobstructed water. I delicately reeled him closer as Ernie readied the net. That was when the bass took a final dive straight down, then shot out of the water like a launched rocket. Despite my desperate reeling, my line slackened. With a shake of his oversized head and, I swear, a grin, the fish spit the weedless right into the boat. And this time I saw exactly what was so different about him.

Ernie and I sat in the boat and watched the last ripples of my struggle disappear. The remains of an angel fire sunset dimmed. Across the lake a heron stood silhouetted at the edge of the bog. I shivered, suddenly chilled through. We pulled the boat out, made our way back through the swamp. Though Ernie had no compass, only the diminishing twilight to guide him, sure enough we reached the high ground and came out precisely at the truck. The damp smell of sweat and swamp filled the cab. We drove home in silence.

All the way back, I kept seeing that fish. I wanted to ask Ernie, to make sure of what I saw, but I could tell he didn't feel like talking. He got out at the store without so much as a good-bye. When I arrived home, Sean, he's my boy, came out of his bedroom and yawned, "Where were you, Daddy?"

"Lard Lake."

"Where's that."

"Near Ella's inlet. Do you know where that is?"

Ernie never did give his notice. His big toe got run over by a full shopping cart and he doesn't walk too well, but he's giving those bags a quarter-turn again. With that toe and all, I doubt he'll ever make it back to Lard Lake. I don't think I'll fish it either, though, not while Ernie's still alive. When he's gone, then it'll be my turn. I'll drive out there, drag the boat through that god-forsaken swamp, row over to the beaver house, and cast a Stanley Weedless. Who knows? I might get lucky and hook a monster bass. If I do, I'll play him till he jumps, then I'll look at him real carefully. Especially the eyes. To see if they're laughing, and they're blue. Then again, maybe next time they'll be green.

Bill Stokes *grew up in northwest Wisconsin, a landscape of forests, rocky pastures and, most important, trout water. Bill was introduced to that water by relatives and friends in a way that left him permanently "trout impaired." After graduating from the University of Wisconsin, Bill began his newspaper career at Stevens Point. He later was an outdoor writer and columnist in Madison and Milwaukee, and wound up his newspaper days with ten years at* The Chicago Tribune. *Bill has authored two children's books, and his newspaper work has been compiled into three books, most recently* The River Is Us, *a collection of nature essays published by Northword Press.*

Published by permission of the author.

To Shoot a Musky

BILL STOKES

---

*Satchel was the undisputed king
of the resident muskies. He had roamed
the flowage for years, periodically
terrorizing innocent fishermen by surfacing
like a whale so close to a boat that
the occupants could look deep into the
fish's black eyes and see what seemed to be
undiluted piscatorial evil.*

I never blamed Uncle Charlie for what happened that day on the Couderay flowage. It was an accident — I think. But it would have been interesting to know just how big that musky was. And I have never been able to figure out if Uncle Charlie really wanted to know, too, or if the musky was more valuable to him as a phantom-like monster that would forever defy man and measurement, perhaps as Nessie is to the people around Loch Ness.

Uncle Charlie was not really my uncle. He was my mother's uncle, but everyone called him Uncle Charlie and so that is what I called him, too. He was an older man by the time I came along, and from the first time I saw him I was fascinated by the craggy, outdoor look of him and by the smell of gun oil and dried pelts that always preceded him and advertised that when he wasn't guiding musky fishermen, he was a gun trader and a fur buyer. In my youthful mind, this put him in a class with Daniel Boone and Davy Crocket, and it was a long time before I could relate to him with anything but slack-jawed adulation.

Uncle Charlie spent a lot of time around the little cross-roads town of Radisson where one of his daughters lived and where his sister, Martha Helsing, and her family operated Helsing's Tavern. Radisson, in northwest Wisconsin, is on the edge of the Chequamegon National Forest, not far from the confluence of the Chippewa and Couderay rivers, which puts it close to some of the world's best musky water. The current world record musky — sixty-nine pounds, eleven ounces — was taken out of the Chippewa flowage back in 1949 by Louie Spray fishing off a sand bar just a twenty-minute drive from Radisson.

But Uncle Charlie's water was the Couderay flowage, a small impoundment that had sprawled over some of the rocky land and boggy marshes when a dam was put across the Couderay river. And he knew it well, down to the location of every sunken log and all of the deep holes that had been old gravel pits before the dam went in.

Most of Uncle Charlie's clients were high rollers from the big cities, and Uncle Charlie had brought enough of them face to face with big, ugly fish to have built a reputation for knowing his business. I once heard him say that his biggest kick was putting one of those city dudes so close to a charging musky that the fisherman had to concentrate on his sphincter muscles to avoid acute embarrassment. Of course, Uncle Charlie didn't say it that way, being prone to more direct language.

Uncle Charlie liked to tell about the fisherman from Chicago who was a member of the Capone gang that came to the Wisconsin woods to "rest up" from the pressures of the liquor business back in the 1920s. This fellow hired Uncle Charlie to take him out after musky, and they were crossing a sand bar when one of the big bobbers went down. As Uncle Charlie told it, when he reached casually down into his tackle box and took out the revolver that he routinely used to dispatch big fish, the Capone client went crazy.

"He thought I was going to gun him down," Uncle Charlie said, "and he told me I could have his new Packard sedan if I would spare his life."

Nobody will ever know just how much of this was gospel — there were those who said that Uncle Charlie had been known to challenge veracity — but he was driving a Packard sedan the first time I remember seeing him.

And he was carrying a revolver, a .32 caliber Smith and Wesson that was always in one of his pockets when it wasn't in the bottom of his tackle box. He seemed to have developed a gunfighter-like attachment to the handgun, taking it with him even on the rare burial/baptism occasions when he made it to church.

The revolver put a sag in the right-hand pocket of his old brown overcoat as he sat slouched in a rear pew, and because he kept the revolver well lubricated, it strengthened the faint, sweet smell of gun oil that hung about him and which was not offensive in a rural community, where animal smells invaded virtually every aspect of life, including the churches. There was, it seemed to me, much more prestige in smelling like a gun rather than a cow, economics notwithstanding.

A game warden once asked Uncle Charlie why he carried the revolver, and Uncle Charlie, a Norwegian, said, "Well, you never know when you might run into a Swede."

When I finally got old enough to finagle a musky fishing trip with Uncle Charlie, he was, to put it kindly, in the twilight of his guiding prowess. Arthritis had put permanent crimps in his rowing arms, and there was a little osteoporosis hump to his spine, as if his long outdoor years had transformed themselves into an uncomfortable little backpack. But Charlie was not ready for life's inevitable grand portage. Not by a long shot. He might have grunted and groaned a little over the effort of getting into the boat, but he wasn't about to let anyone else do the rowing, and he hadn't forgotten a detail of the river's underwater character, nor any of the musky haunts.

That memorable day that I went out with him was soft and gray, the kind that was good for musky fishing, according to Uncle Charlie. As he rowed us away from shore, he announced that we were going to have some action.

Might even raise ol' Satchel," he said. "It's about time for him to feed again."

If Uncle Charlie was the dean of Couderay flowage musky guides, Satchel — short for Satchelass — was the undisputed king of the resident muskies. He (though the big fish was probably a she, everyone referred to it as he) had roamed the flowage for years, periodically terrorizing innocent fishermen by smashing their tackle and occasionally surfacing like a whale so close to a boat that the occupants could look deep into the fish's black eyes and see what seemed to be undiluted piscatorial evil. Such experiences were always good for business up at Helsing's Tavern, where the respective fishermen would retreat to restore their shattered nerves.

Uncle Charlie had tangled with the big fish so many times that there had developed a Captain Ahab/Moby Dick relationship. "I'll get him before I die," Uncle Charlie would say. "And if I don't I'm comin' back."

We were half way around the flowage, gliding slowly past a rock outcrop to the rhythmic squeak of the oarlocks, when my bobber suddenly disappeared.

"Could be him," Uncle Charlie said. "He hangs out here sometimes."

I could feel my heart start to pound, erratically, like a rat trying desperately to leap out of an empty garbage can, and I watched the water where the bobber had been with a curious mix of fear and anticipation. What if it was Satchel? What if the legendary old monster was out there mouthing my sucker bait and preparing to take me on? I was not up to it. I had no experience. I had never even caught an undersized musky. It would be better if the bobber popped to the surface and we could troll peacefully on down the shoreline.

You might as well put down your rod and relax," Uncle Charlie said, stroking the oars gently to hold the boat in place. "It takes a musky at least half an hour to turn a sucker around and swallow it. We'll give him plenty of time."

Him! Him? Did Uncle Charlie really think it was Satchel? It was very quiet, just the distant buzz of an engine somewhere off toward Radisson and the vacant cawing of a crow. Time stopped and then went backwards. I wanted to ask Uncle Charlie a hundred questions, but that would only have emphasized the extent of my amateur standing. This was no time for that.

Uncle Charlie smoked a cigarette, and then another one, and he seemed as calm as a bluegill fisherman.

I reached down for the fishing rod, and Uncle Charlie said, "Not yet. It's only been fifteen minutes."

Fifteen minutes, hell! It had been fifteen hours!

"First we'll ease the line tight," Uncle Charlie said, "and then you set the hook. And set it with everything you've got. Reef back two or three times, and then keep the line tight."

It sounded simple enough, but a strange twitching had developed between my shoulder blades, and I was not sure my arms would function. Also, my eyes didn't seem to be focusing sharply.

Finally, Uncle Charlie told me to pick up the rod and slowly reel in the line until all the slack was out of it. I went about it like a zombie, shaking, sweating and hyperventilating. Then the line was taut, and Uncle Charlie said, "Now!"

I brought the rod back with all my strength, and the line snapped tight. I thought it must be snagged to an underwater stump, because there had not been the slightest give to it. I felt some relief, and then realized that Uncle Charlie was shouting, "Hit him again! Hit him again!"

I hauled back on the rod a second time, and then, way out where the bobber had disappeared, the water erupted in a volcanic explosion around a giant fish that hung over the bruised surface for just a second before splashing back beneath the radiating circles of waves. The size of the fish and its violent appearance pretty much destroyed me, shattering any capacity for calculated activity and seriously damaging even basic reflexes. Uncle Charlie was shouting, but I couldn't make out what he was saying as I waved the rod around like a drunken flag bearer and turned the reel handle backwards so that a big tangle of line developed. Somehow, the line straightened itself out, and then all I could do was hang on with clenched muscles as the musky alternately towed us around the flowage and made several more heart-stopping leaps.

It was a tremendous fish, appearing to be as long as the boat and with a mouth that seemed to open wide enough to swallow up a deer.

I don't know how long the fight went on. It seemed like hours, and my muscles began to jerk and ache with sudden cramps. Uncle Charlie gave continuous advice about how much tension to keep on the fish and when to reel in or let out line.

"It's him," he said at one point. "I've been fishing for him for years."

An uncomfortable aura of involvement in something far beyond my meager capacities enveloped me, and I alternately vowed to myself that I would never go musky fishing again, and then that I would spend the rest of my life at it.

He's tiring," Uncle Charlie said, and I glanced over to see him reach down into his tackle box for his revolver. I pulled harder on the fish and felt it give enough so that I gained a few feet of line. And then after several false surrenders when the musky came slowly past us only to swim off again, the mammoth old lunker was finally just beneath the surface alongside the boat. Its size was unbelievable, and all I could think of was how there couldn't possibly be room for us and the fish in the same boat, especially a boat as small as Uncle Charlie's old wooden skiff.

"Shoot him! Shoot him!" I shouted, and looked quickly at Uncle Charlie to see him sitting slouched between the oars, his eyes focused on the fish, his mouth slightly open. As if it were a dream with everything in slow motion, I watched as he slowly raised his revolver.

And then with the sound of the shot, the pressure on my line was so abruptly released that I nearly fell over backwards. As I regained my balance I could see the piece of broken line dangling from my rod. It had been cleanly severed by Uncle Charlie's bullet, and I looked at him in disbelief.

Uncle Charlie was still staring down at the big musky, and I, too, looked at the fish as it lay still for a few seconds and then, very slowly, with a strange dignity, sank into the tannin-colored water and disappeared.

"He broke off," Uncle Charlie said finally.

But ... "

"You should've given him some line."

Give him some line? My god, Uncle Charlie's bullet had given him all of the line. But Uncle Charlie was apparently not going to see it that way, not for my benefit, anyway. I wanted to ask Uncle Charlie how he could have missed the fish at such close range, and why it had taken him so long to shoot, and why in hell he had been so dumb as to shoot off my line. But I kept my mouth shut.

"It was him," Uncle Charlie said. "Mean as ever."

We didn't fish much after that. Uncle Charlie seemed to have lost his zest for it, and I was emotionally drained and ready to call it a day. As we gathered up the gear and stowed the boat, it seemed to me that Uncle Charlie was unusually cheerful for a man who had just been a party to losing what was undoubtedly a record fish.

"You're young," he said, apparently sensing my disappointment. "You'll get more chances at the big ones."

And then he took the revolver out of his tackle box and slipped it into a pants pocket as we headed for the car.

Many years later, I dropped into Helsing's Tavern, and there on the wall behind the bar was what appeared to be a giant musky. A small sign labeled the fish as Satchelass.

Bob Helsing, Uncle Charlie's nephew, was tending bar, and he said the fish was not a real mount but had been carved from a big pine log by one of Uncle Charlie's grown grandchildren. It was very skillfully done and had been painted to be as lifelike as any mounted fish ever could be. Bob said the fish had been structured according to dimensions given by Uncle Charlie just before he died, and it represented a fish much larger than Louie Spray's record catch. No sign of the real Satchelass had been seen since Uncle Charlie's death, Bob added.

We hear vague reports now and then," Bob said with a grin. "One fellow who lives on the flowage even says that on foggy days he still hears the squeak of Uncle Charlie's oarlocks, so maybe both him and the big fish are still out there."

Of course they are. And I'll bet a round for the house that Uncle Charlie still has his revolver with him.

Gordon MacQuarrie *(1900-56) was outdoor editor of* The Milwaukee Journal *from 1936 until his death. His name is attached to Wisconsin's highest outdoor writer's recognition, The Gordon MacQuarrie Award, presented annually by the Wisconsin Academy of Sciences, Arts and Letters. His famous stories of The Old Duck Hunters' Association, Inc., appeared in* The Journal *and in national outdoor magazines from the 1930s to 1950s. Most are set in northwestern Wisconsin. The Old Duck Hunters stories, featuring Hizzoner Mr. President (actually MacQuarrie's father-in-law) and himself, have been compiled in what is known as the MacQuarrie Trilogy, available from Willow Creek Press of Minocqua, Wis. The ODHA, of course, did more than just pursue ducks. Fly Fishing With MacQuarrie, another Willow Creek title, recounts memorable moments on the Brule River and other trout streams.*

Now, in June

GORDON MacQUARRIE

You are as relaxed, physically
and mentally, as you will ever be.
The river has reached out like an old friend
and made a place for you. You pack
a leisurely pipe, and the water about you
is lit for a minute, the match hisses
in the river and the babbling mystery
of the night deepens.

---

*N*o time is better for trout fishermen than early June. Other months may approach it. They may even excel it now and then. But what I am getting at is that June is the best time for trout fishermen, as well as trout fishing.

Take the President of the Old Duck Hunters' Association, Inc., for instance. This symbolic angler said to me one night in knee-deep June in his back yard, "I can tell by the smell in the air I am going trout fishing tomorrow."

It was a good smell. Flowers were coming up out of brown earth. Insects hummed. The neighborhood was suffused with the odors of lush June. You smelled it and, smelling it, wondered if you would take those stuffy waders tomorrow or just an old pair of pants for wading.

"Yes, sir," said Mr. President, "I can smell trout tonight. I can smell 'em along towards tomorrow night on the Namakagon below Cable. I will just put me in there at Squaw Bend for maybe not more 'n and hour or two. It'll be dusk when the wind dies, so the mosquitoes will help me change flies.

"First, I will eat supper in the car. I will be pretty lazy about it. I will not be hurried, you understand? I will set there a spell. I'll bet I hardly move a muscle until I hear the first whip-poor-will. Then after a bit I will jump in below the county trunk bridge and tempt providence and the good brown trout of the Namakagon with large, unscientific, come-sundown flies. That is what I will do."

Imagine a man in this feverish age, twenty-four hours beforehand, declaring exactly what he will do twenty-four hours hence, come what will as to weather, business or the current status of his sciatic rheumatism.

"Yep," he reiterated there in his back yard. "I will drive down past McKinney's drug store there in Cable and over to the river, and just as I'm arriving at Squaw Bend four cars with Illinois license plates will be pulling out. These will be city fishermen who don't know any better than to fish for Namakagon browns in broad daylight. They will be sore at the river. They will tell me there ain't a brown in the river — never was! They will go away from there, leaving it to me just when I want it, as the fishing gets good.

"I'm danged if I can figger out what trout fishermen these days are thinking about. They start at 10 a.m. after a good night's rest and a leisurely breakfast. They fish until the six o'clock whistle and wonder why they don't get 'em. People like that are not entitled to catch trout. To catch trout, you got to suffer and learn."

He carried out the next day's schedule to a T. He abandoned his business at three, and one hour later came up my front walk in khaki trousers, his eyes snapping. I was only half ready. There had been a slight argument at our house. My wife, who is Mister President's daughter, just sort of hung around and looked abused while I picked up my stuff. That can unnerve people like me.

The President took in matters at a glance and yelped, "For heaven's sake, woman! Get away from that man. Can't you see he ain't soaked his leaders yet?"

Think of it! A man who can talk like that and make it stick! Picking up the final odds and ends, however, I wondered for the hundredth time why he could not command so imperiously in his own house, where he achieves his ends by other means — obsequiousness, if not downright chicanery. It's a smart man who knows when he's licked.

"Trout fishing is not like drinking beer," he lectured as the car sped south and east. "It's more like sipping champagne. A good beer drinker just sits him down and lays into it. You hear the first one splash. But you just sip champagne. You take a tiny leetle bit and smack your lips.

"So with trout. You don't want too many. You want to get the stage all set. You look ahead and figger out every move. You will not be rushed. You are not after a bait of fish. If you are, you would go down to the St. Croix and jerk the derned teeth out of smallmouths. What you are after is to fool a trout, or maybe four or five.

"I'm for filling frying pans, you understand. But only now and then. More often I'm for picking out a trout so smart he thinks he's running for the legislature. There he is, living under the bank by daylight and sneering at the guys who waste their time working over him when the sun is high. My idea of perfection is to give that guy a dose of sprouts — to teach him a lesson he won't forget, if I can't creel him."

"Then you have some places in mind ... "

"I'll thank you not to poke into other people's affairs and also to stay away from that hole two hundred yards below the town road, where the big dead stump sticks out into the river."

"Agreed. In return, will you avoid the fast rip below the island?"

"Why should I fool with half-pounders?" he snorted. "Your ten-cent rips are secure against trespass."

We drove under Cable's gorgeous pines, past McKinney's drug store, which has seen more big browns than most drug stores, past the sawmill, and thence to the Namakagon at Squaw Bend, which is some place.

"Not exactly slightly known, however," Mister President replied when I raised the question. "Too doggone well known. But happily, not intimately to fishermen who will play its own game."

"Like who?"

"Like me. Me, I wouldn't come down here a-whipping and a-lashing this crick in broad daylight. Oh, mebbe I would on an overcast, windy day. And how many of those do we get in a season? Me, I'd come down here either first thing in the morning or last thing at night. I'd rather do this than mow the lawn, I would ... "

He wheeled the car across a shallow, dry ditch, and it settled on low, hard ground, off the road. Twenty feet away the Namakagon journeyed by in the last direct rays of the sun. He broke out sandwiches and coffee and forbade me to move out of the car "until the time is ripe."

There was the dear old river. And sure enough, two disgusted fishermen coming to their car, parked nearby, who answered a hail with "You can have our share of it."

"Imagine!" snorted the President. "The exalted conceit of people who will fish this creek on a day the sky is so bright it isn't blue, but white! There they go, and fair weather after them. Quitting at seven o'clock. You know, I think this present generation of trout fishermen is afraid of the dark!"

Softly comes the night along the Namakagon. Born in cold, crooked-shored Namakagon Lake, it curves south and west to the St. Croix, its upper reaches trout water, its lower reaches smallmouth water almost on a par with the St. Croix itself.

There it was, just beyond the car windows, gray and ropy in the growing dusk. It ran under the county trunk bridge, surged to the right and lost itself around the corner, where there is a grand series of rips. You just look at that kind of river in June and want to plump right into it.

Not, however, when the President is in charge. We sat and munched. In that far northern corner of Wisconsin, darkness comes slowly in early June. That is a great help to deliberate evening campaigners. Those twilights were made for trout fishermen. They give you time, the President says, "to square off at it."

It was a night to remember, and the Old Duck Hunters remember many such and are properly thankful that June along the Namakagon is a month of heavy perfumes and many birds. No stretch of the Namakagon in the Cable-Seeley country offers more than the Squaw Bend territory.

Trout waters can be very personal places. The best trout streams are the ones you grow up with and then grow old with. Eventually they become like a familiar shotgun, or a faithful old setter, or a comfortable pair of shoes. You develop a profound affection for them, and you think maybe before you die you will even understand a little about them.

We went downstream, he on the right bank, I on the left. At this putting-in place, high above the right bank, stretches the level top of an old logging railroad grade. The light was waning in the west, and the top of this embankment cut off the sky like a knife. Below this ran the churning river, far noisier and more mysterious than it had been an hour before.

Certainly you must know how it is to come to a place like this. A place you know well. A place where you are on intimate terms with the smallest boulders, where yonder projecting limb once robbed you of a choice fly, where from beneath the undercut banks the big ones prowl by night to claim the larger morsels of the darkness.

Strange and utterly irresistible are such places to trout fishermen. There you had hold of a good one. Here you netted a smaller one. Down beyond the turn in the pool below the old snag pile you lost still another. The spell of the approaching night silenced the President, but not for long.

"One thing I can't figger out," he said finally. His voice came to me from a point downstream, drifting over the purring waters in the sweet June air, "How can a Scotch Presbyterian like you enjoy anything that's so much fun?"

He vanished in the gloom like some wise and ancient spirit of the river. I heard his wader brogues nick a rock as he stumbled, heard him cuss softly, and then the river took me in ...

Though it is early June, the mosquitoes are not bad. One of those rare nights when the pesky hordes fail to discover you there in mid-river. The temperature has dropped quickly from a sunlit eighty or so to below seventy, and you know it will be a night for blankets. You know, too, as the water laps at waders that it is the cool, kindly hand of night which chills your river every twenty-four hours and makes it livable for trout.

You are as relaxed, physically and mentally, as you will ever be. The river has reached out like an old friend and made a place for you. You pack a leisurely pipe, and the water about you is lit for a minute, the match hisses in the river and the babbling mystery of the night deepens.

The current picks at your knees. Your fingers feel in the darkness for the familiar shapes of bass-sized trout flies. A whim will decide which one. From long experience you have learned to hold fingers toward the western sky as you bend on your choice.

What to do? Work the right bank down, foot by foot, with the short, efficient line of the after-sunset angler? Or cover all the water methodically, persistently?

Plop! A Namakagon brown has decided the issue for you. He is downstream maybe as much as fifty yards, and a good fat plop it is. Just the kind of trout you would expect to come prowling out from the snags on a cool June evening. You know it is the careless fling of a worthy brown, and you are pretty sure he will look at something big and buggy, that he is confident and bellicose.

But just a minute now! You've tried these fish before in the near dark. They come quickly and they go quickly. Once pricked, they standeth not upon the ceremony of their departing. You tighten up a bit. Browns, though more foolhardy by night, can still be very chancy. You do, however, reach around and feel for the net handle, but quickly make personal amends to whatever fishing gods there be. You know it does not pay to be cocky. You know you must study to be humble and alert.

You take it easy in getting to a spot upstream from the fish. You get over to the left bank for your little stalk, and you lift your feet high and put them down easily. You study the vague outline of the branches with which you will have to contend in casting. You take long, hard drags at the little blackened pipe, so that the bowl glows hot. You are on edge and ready. You get within thirty-five feet of the place and wait ...

Plop! Goos! He is not frightened. You false-cast with the big fly, wondering how to show it to him. A slack-line drift down over him? Or a cross-current cast and a smart retrieve? You decide on the former. It will disturb the water less, and you can come back to the fussier cast later.

You lengthen line, and you know your fly is going over his window. Nothing. Again and again you cast, letting it drift below him and out into midstream. And you retrieve each time carefully, so as not to whip his top water and frighten him. Still nothing. He isn't seeing it.

Very well. You have covered all the corners of his window with the dead floating fly. You have shown him Business No. 1, and he wants none of it. Very well. Now for action, à la bass stream. Zip, zip, zip! The fly is brought back over his window in short jerks.

Ka-doong! That was the medicine. He's got it. He's fast and he's heavy and he's going places. Now, for Pete's sake, take it easy. The leader is sound and the stream is free of stuff, except for that undercut bank. He is bucking like a mule. You strip in a couple of feet, tentatively, and exult at your strategy in showing him an actionable fly, something struggling and toothsome.

He's certainly husky. Those Namakagon browns are built like tugboats. He's sidewise now, below you, in midstream, giving you the works. He has broken water a couple times. He rushes you, and you strip like mad, letting the retrieved line fall where it may in the current.

And then after you have given him Mister President's "dose of sprouts," and you reach around and feel the hickory handle of the net …

Like many another after dark brown on the Namakagon, this one was a good pound and a half. I did not see him until he was in the net, and that is unusual. Generally, you see living flashes of fleshy brown out there in the gloom. He was reddish and thick and cold as ice as I removed the fly, tapped him on the head and slid him into the wide, deep jacket pocket I use for a creel.

I was trembling. I can't take 'em without quaking. They get right down under me and turn flip-flops inside. The pipe was out. The stripped line was bellied downstream. The fly was chewed. It was a pattern evolved by a friend whose stamping ground is the surging Wolf River. A few of its devotees gave it a name a year back — Harvey Alft's Nonpareil — and it has stuck.

I went over and sat on a boulder near the bank. Just one trout — and all that fuss. I sat and wondered, as all men have, if the day would ever come when I could take so small a fraction of a trout stream's population and not develop a galloping pulse.

I have caught more trout than I deserve to catch. And always and forever, the good ones like this fellow put me on edge, send me hippity-hopping to a boulder or the bank to sit down and gather my wits.

Another pipeful helped settle things. I thought, sitting there, another bold trout might betray himself by leaping, but none did. I tested the leader, smoked out the pipe and went back upstream by the left bank. Now the first plan of campaign would be in order — fish the right bank like a machine. Swish-swish. That was the only sound there in the dark as the Nonpareil sailed back and out, back and out. Maybe there would be one or two right in close to the bank, just outside the protecting roots.

There was. Indeed there was. Another golden-bellied Namakagon brown mouthed Harvey Alft's Nonpareil with sure determination and made for midstream and faster water. He was smaller, but lively. I horsed him a bit. You are permitted to do that when you are building up to a brace. A pair is so much better than a loner. Two more were netted through the methodical casting toward the right bank, out from which they lay feeding. And there is little excuse for repeating the old, old story.

It was getting on toward 10 p.m., which is the time you quit on trout streams in Wisconsin. I moved downstream to the sacred precincts of Mister President's pool. The whip-poor-wills were in a dither. A deer splashed at the stream bank and snorted back through the brush. The flat top of the old logging grade was now lit by the stars.

I was proud of my fish. I showed them to him. He said they were fish that would disgrace no man's skillet. He was sitting on the bank in the dark. His glowing cigar end attracted me. He was a little weary, and I felt a little guilty when he pounded me on the back and then said he had nothing — "but I had hold of one — the one!"

Nothing for Mister President. I do not like to wind up trout trips with him that way. And, in all conscience, I seldom do!

We followed the bank back to the car and pulled off our waders. It was just ten o'clock. He slumped a little over the wheel, for he was beaten and he was tired. And then, before he stepped on the starter, he rolled down a window and took a good, long sniff of the Namakagon's June aroma.

"You know," he said, "I can tell by the smell in the air that I am going trout fishing tomorrow."

In the strange half-light that
precedes the dawn, you load the skiffs
and shove off. Largely by instinct,
you paddle to your blind. In the east,
the dawn is wrestling with the night
on a mat of low-hanging clouds.

The result is a blood-red draw.
A shot off in the distance marks the
opening hour. You hunker down in
the cattails and scan the sky.

CLAY SCHOENFELD
From "Memo About Mallards"

Chuck Petrie *left Wisconsin in 1994 to become an expatriate writer in Memphis, Tenn. When it was pointed out to him that to become an expatriate you actually had to leave your native country, he replied, "Tennessee is a foreign country. Even the food and language are different, y'all. You can bet your grits on it." Chuck is now executive editor at* Ducks Unlimited *magazine. In previous lives he served as managing editor for* Wisconsin Sportsman *magazine, founding editor of* Wisconsin Outdoor Journal, *and editor of* Wisconsin Outdoor News. *An ardent waterfowl hunter and fly fisherman, he lives in Cordova, Tenn., with wife Mary and their eight-year-old Labrador retriever, Gunnar. The three make regular trips to their Wisconsin homeland each year.*

Reprinted by permission of the author. This essay first appeared in Wildfowl Magazine.

Reflections on a Wood Duck Pond

CHUCK PETRIE

*Reflections on a wood duck pond seem
to take the harshness out of reality.
Here, where there is just still water
and solitude, my mind follows time
in any direction, and I can believe that
all is right in my life, that the future
will be gentle, and my past,
when necessary, has been forgiven.*

Giving up a secure job with the government and a low-interest G.I. mortgage on a new home in the suburbs may sound like a screwy thing to do, especially for a thirty-nine-year-old man with a wife and children. But it was a decision my wife and I made three years ago, and we don't regret it — most of the time. We wanted a challenge, something different. We wanted to live in the country, where we would be free of the problems of living on the rim of a city. Besides, I needed a change from the tedium of a mindless, paper-shuffling bureaucracy.

And on evenings when I sit in my canoe, nestled in the bulrush cover on this wood duck pond, waiting for birds to fly over the tree line before they buzz the water on their pre-roosting security sweep, I don't regret the decision one bit.

I am alone on the pond, four acres of quiet water bordered by autumn-gold tamarack and surrounded by cattail and bulrush. I know the ducks will come. They do almost every night in the first three weeks of October. They are predictable. It is almost not fair, I feel, that I take advantage of their predictability. That is why I come here only four or five times a season, and shoot no more than one wood duck each time, and sometimes none. I am rich here. I can have a duck almost any night I want one. It depends on my whims. I meditate on this power and am frightened by it.

I put out only a half-dozen decoys — four mallards and, well to one side, a pair of wood duck blocks. The woodies invariably head for that treacherous pair, and sometimes they come in so fast I don't even get a chance to shoot. Then I watch the meeting of the newcomers and their plastic brethren. Usually the encounter is short-lived, and the ducks, betrayed, will swim away or fly a short distance to another part of the pond. It is amusing but deceitful.

Wood ducks are not the only waterfowl that come to the pond. When the wind blows hard from the east, the big lake, only a few miles away, is churned into froth. Then mallards might come, or bluebills or ringnecks. But they are different, and I feel no compunction about shooting at these transients.

And there are other birds. Sometimes a blue heron will stalk the shallow border of the pond. Migrating geese sometimes fly over and, although I know they see the pond and sometimes gabble among themselves as if discussing a possible resting place, they evidently disagree on its suitability and continue south. I occasionally hear a grouse drumming in the thick, dark halo of woods that surrounds the water, and I know there are migrating woodcock out there, too.

I don't hunt the grouse and woodcock. My agreement with the man who owns the pond is that I only hunt ducks. That's okay. I have many other places to hunt grouse and woodcock and, for that matter, ducks. But this is a special place. It is only three miles from my home. The landowner lets me keep my canoe in the woods near the edge of the pond, so I can leave my house and set up here in just minutes. There is a farm a half-mile away from the pond.

And yet, except for the occasional bellow of a cow, when its udder is turgid at milking time, or the sight of a white contrail against the blue sky, I can imagine myself in the wilderness. This little lake is spring fed, and some day it will be a bog. Even now there are pitcher plants growing on the damp, wooded trail leading to the water's edge, and spongy bog moss is beginning to infiltrate the cattails. This pond could be in northern Minnesota, Quebec or Alaska, and sometimes I let my imagination convince me that I'm hunting in one of those places.

There is a stream flowing from the pond, but the beavers have dammed it. This year, consequently, the water level is high, and the water spills over into the woods on the lower sides of the basin to the west and north. Some afternoons I can hear wood ducks calling, their shrill ascending whistles echoing from back in the trees.

The beavers' lodge is on the southwest shore. They have free run of the pond from there and are not afraid to swim right into my decoys. Inquisitive animals, a pair will often come snooping around the blocks, inspecting them. Invariably, one will slap its tail on the water to express his disapproval of these strange objects, then swim away to pursue more serious endeavors.

On the west shore, two hundred yards north of the beaver lodge, lie the half-submerged remains of an old blind. Whoever built it went to great lengths to ensure comfortable hunting. It consists of two-by-fours and plywood with a roof. The sides are covered with tarpaper, and the roof is shingled. Inside, the blind had room for three hunters to sit and shoot out of the large open port that faces the pond. Now, though, the blind sits cockeyed in the water, its wood rotted, its shingles brittle with age and exposure to the heat and cold.

Occasionally I find myself staring at this decrepit blind, wondering about the people who hunted it. Who were they? Where are they now? When did they build the blind? I entertain myself by making up answers to these questions and envisioning three men sitting in the blind as it appeared years ago. The hunters look like they stepped off the cover of a sporting magazine from the 1930s. Two of the men have '97 Winchesters leaning against the wall of the blind; the other cradles a double-barrel — a weathered A.H. Fox — in his arms.

The men's shells are paper and brass, and the decoys in the water in front of them are wood. Squeezed between two of the hunters on the blind's board seat is a Labrador retriever, looking forward, his eyes fixed on the empty space above the wooden blocks. Perhaps this dog was a distant sire of the old Lab sitting in the bow of my canoe. I imagine that dog sitting among the men, and then I look at my dog and notice that he, too, is staring at the blind, his brown eyes lost in concentration.

There are brook trout in this pond; I know it. Actually, I don't really know they are in the pond itself, but I know the outlet stream holds brook trout. It only stands to reason that the pond would have them, too; it is cold and deep, except for the shallow rim that supports the cattails and bulrushes. I've never tried to fish for the trout. I am afraid if I tried, I might not catch any and decide there weren't any here. It's comforting to think the trout are here, and I'd like to keep it that way.

It is getting dark on the pond now. Shooting is allowed until sunset, but the pond, in a basin and surrounded by trees, sees night early. The tree line is slowly eclipsing the sun, and the shadow of the tamaracks is crossing the water. When the dark veil reaches the other side and ascends to the opposite tree line, the entire basin will be enveloped in shadow. Still, it will be legal to shoot for another twenty minutes, until the sun sets.

It's time to anticipate the arrival of the wood ducks, but instead I look over the side of the canoe, into the water, at my reflection. My slight movement causes a series of tiny swells to radiate from the hull, distorting my image.

This leisure is one of the beauties of being alone in a duck blind. It allows me time to meditate, to relax and see things in other perspectives, to soften the images of the past, present and future. Reflections on a wood duck pond seem to take the harshness out of reality — not necessarily distorting it but softening it, at least temporarily. Sitting on the bank of a stream, watching the current go by, I often get a helpless feeling of being left behind in time. Here, though, where there is no current, just still water and solitude, my mind follows time in any direction, and I can believe that all is right in my life, that the future will be gentle, and my past, when necessary, has been forgiven.

Now it is too late to shoot. This will be a clear night, and the ducks won't come in before dusk the way they do on cloudy, overcast afternoons. So, in the gathering darkness, I paddle out to the decoys, pick them up, and head for shore. But before I can beach the canoe the ducks arrive. They haven't disappointed me. In flocks of five and ten they come in low, fast, circling the edge of the pond before finally pitching in toward the center of the circle of dark water. The dog and I sit quietly in the canoe and watch until it is too dark to see anymore.

Dick Yatzeck, *of Bear Creek, teaches Russian literature at Lawrence University in Appleton "in order to buy dog food and 20-gauge shells." He also writes literature in English for outdoor magazines and is working on a set of stories about hunting in southern Russia. A volume of tales modeled on Turgenev's* Sportsman's Sketches *should appear shortly in the trade list of the University of Wisconsin Press. The stories in that collection mostly appeared in* The Ruffed Grouse Society *magazine and in* Wisconsin Outdoor Journal.

Too Hasty for Coon

DICK YATZECK

There is a primal, ancient, smoky joy in running coon, but the tempo is set by the coon and the hounds, not by the hunters. This was hard on Steve, who liked to drive fast cars and use two telephones at once.

I suppose it must have been October. I'd finished college, had my first teaching job, and was looking for a place, an occasion, to hunt. It was October.

My only connection in that neck of the woods was Steve, a former student of mine in Madison, a smart, restless fellow raised on the Wolf River. He planned to have his first million by the time he hit thirty-five and was turning over real estate like a skunk upending rocks for grubs, but could maybe just spare a quick evening for the hounds. He took me to the Boecks farm.

Now my friend Steve was restless, even pushy, but Rhiney Boecks, a deer hunting buddy of Steve's dad, was as hard to push as a hay rope. When we got there it was still light. Steve left the car at a trot. Rhiney had finished the chores, but now he was ready for a little talkin' and spittin', and after that, there were the chickens.

Rhiney's chickens seemed to be all over the acreage. A random redbone hound and some rusty chicken wire had led to a poultry breakout and, as we sat spittin', the apple orchard was filling up with cornish cross meat chickens going to roost. They had to be gathered safe from the mink before Rhiney would set a dog on track.

We gathered. We climbed apple trees. Rhiney and his boys worked slow and easy, and the chickens hardly stirred in their sleep. Steve and I plucked down nine-pound, squawking, defecating hens and seven-pound roosters whose wings beat like barn boards. I groped clumsily and had a couple of ripped thumbs for my trouble. Steve snatched chickens out of the tress until hell wouldn't have it, caught a bloody nose and a fairly purple eye, but got the job done. He must have brought in fifty by himself.

"Now, let's go," he said.

"Well," said Rhiney, "the dogs are in the loose box in the barn. We can take a look." Those hounds, two bluetick and the errant redbone — Tracey, Ranter and Fox — rang like heavy bells at the sight of Rhiney in the evening. In the loose box, which connected with an outside run through a hole cut in the side of the barn, their eyes glowed green and electric, and taut haunches and torn ears spoke of readiness and experience. They looked like chasers.

We didn't look long. Steve threw a sack with climbing irons liberated from the telephone company over his shoulder. One of his schemes was to catch a pair of young coons, breed them and start a fur farm. Rhiney collected a .22 single shot and a lantern out of the mud room. Rhiney's boys, as many as there were dogs, pulled on hip boots and thrust leashes into their pockets. We were ready.

"But hey, how 'bout some medsun?" said Rhiney. "Some o' that piss from the sick horse."

"Oh, cripes," muttered Steve, reducing his gallop to a trot as we came into the oat field above the Boecks slough. But he pulled a pint of Royal Host out of a pocket — he had come prepared — and Rhiney imbibed.

"Now, let's move!" said Steve. But we didn't. We stood in the oat stubble on that little hill and we all imbibed, except Steve. He was no teetotaler, but when he hunted, by criminy, he meant to hunt.

I flopped down on some broken straw bales, forgotten in the fury of harvest. Rhiney drawled, "All right, now the pump's primed."

And just then Fox said "H-u-u-u!" and Ranter said "H-o-o-o!' and the dogs moved like panthers and there was a sliver of moon at most and just a touch of white mist rising in the low spots.

"H-o-o-o!" went Ranter again and "Ha-ha!" went Fox.

"Jeepers that's a nice sound," said Rhiney. He was old enough to say jeepers. He bit off a chew of brown mule.

"How soon'll they tree?" asked Steve.

The joy of it, the special thrill of running with coon hounds, is that it happens at night, in night's different world. Every tree, every bush is new and strange. You hear more when you see less. You imagine the hounds running lynx, cougar, though an old boar coon is quite able to drown a dog or rip up the hand or leg of an incautious hunter. There is a primal, ancient, smoky joy in running coon, but the tempo is set by the coon and the hounds, not by the hunters. This was hard on Steve, who liked to drive fast cars and use two telephones at once.

"Can't we cut around and bushwhack the coon?" Steve pleaded, twenty minutes after boys and dogs had run out of hearing. "Can't we speed this process up some?"

"Well," said Rhiney, "— pass that medsun, will yuh? — when we hear the dogs again we can maybe figger where the coon is headin', but it's best to sit 'til we hear Tracey tree. Tracey trees nice."

Steve, who had yet to sit down, fidgeted until his climbing irons clanked. Then, after some while, "Ho-oo-ee!" went what had to be Tracey. Steve was off the straw pile and going thirty before Rhiney could cap the medsun. "Don't shoot Tracey ... "

VAROOM! Vroom-vruroom-rawrr!

"What in hell is that?"

"Fox Valley Speedway, just over th' hill," Rhiney got out, after five minutes of howling, rusty stock car mufflers had thoroughly deafened us.

"But how can you hear the dogs, then?"

"In between," said Rhiney. "Just in between. I kin hear 'em. I c'ld hear Tracey anywhere."

I am making a story of Steve's impatience, but I myself have become restless. I want to take you right to the tree, the coon, the hounds throbbing as if with current in lantern light.

I don't even have time "in between," as Rhiney said, to really, truly hear the dogs, or to seek them aurally when they are silent. I am also, now, twenty years farther along. Everything, even Christmas, comes, moves faster.

Rhiney and I sauntered down the hill on Steve's hot track. He was long gone, "gone away," as the English say of a fast fox. Rhiney stumbled companionably along under the roar of the race cars, knowing his hounds and land so well that even in the dark, deafened, he had a good idea where the coons had led the dogs. Off ahead of us, across the deep slough that we were circling, Steve was checking treetops for coon eyes with his five-cell light.

"Hasty feller," said Rhiney. "Decent, but hasty. Th' dogs are, maybe, two sloughs over."

The racket of the race cars quit, and again the "Ho!" and "Ha!" of the dogs gladdened the night. Tracey was still barking at tree, "Ho-ee!" But apart from her, beyond her singing, Ranter and Fox seemed to be running a different animal. We had just time to hear Steve splash, at speed, into the second slough and toward the treeing Tracey, when the dragsters started up again. Steve's light bobbed crazily across the water and reeds. He wasn't sauntering.

The car roars were louder this time, maybe because we had come out from the shadow of the hill, and I couldn't talk to Rhiney for the noise. I could think, though. I swished my pacs through frosty oat stubble and then, then ... my hand remembers the tiny, quick flame of stinging nettle, the graininess of frost-nipped deer fern, that grew near the slough willow and swamp maple. My hand's memory is sharp. But I remember, too, that my thought, under the nasty clatter, was sad. I remembered running dogs twenty years before that in quieter times. I thought of the loss of eye and ear space to encroaching concrete and motors, of all the horses, Nel and Sal and Linda, dry bones now, replaced by stinking iron. I was, I am, a stupid romantic. I mourn the loss of the old, quiet country, when you could hear the tinny rattle of deer fern, as I certainly could not that night.

"Medsun!" shouted Rhiney, right against my ear, and I passed him the bottle Steve had forgotten, shared it. The motors stopped then. Tracey was treeing just around a bend of the slough, forepaws braced against the broad trunk of an old, squat swamp maple, the kind that's hard to drop and that tries to drop on you. Good. It was all just right, the chanting dog, Steve swarming up the tree in his irons to catch the coon alive, and close now, finally honoring Tracey's tree, Ranter and Fox closing in, yipping. Coon eyes sparkled just above Steve's climbing light. Four eyes.

"Two cubs," he sang out. "Just let me get the bag over 'em and I'll have my brood stock."

Enterprise was about to triumph. But Rhiney said, "Hold on, Stevie, here come th' ma!" He'd seen what I, concentrated on Steve's success, almost missed.

A child-sized, silver-tipped black ball rolled just past the lantern Rhiney had lit and set down. Ranter and Fox lunged close behind it. The big ball bounced over a maple root and expanded into a forty-pound sow coon, kind of impatient to retrieve the cubs she'd left in the tree for safekeeping. Steve was on her route.

She was up twelve feet of trunk and six feet of Steve before his flashlight hit the ground. She and the cubs splashed into the slough-edge rushes just as Steve, yowling, "Get 'em, Tracey!" impacted on the hard-trodden cow path. Then Tracey, Ranter and Fox blasted off over Steve, who was just rising out of the tangle of his climbing irons. Much of his difficulty was caused by the coon sack that had dropped back over his head as the sow coon swarmed him.

"Well," said Rhiney, as the hounds whopped off after the water-borne coon, "I guess Stevie could use some medsun now." Steve drank. He smoked in the chill air, the slough water boiling off him, and he drank again, and sputtered and coughed and drank.

It was a fair night for coon. We lost those three in the slough, ran two more but never treed, heard a whole symphony of hound music, and thought about Steve and haste. Rhiney was quiet, but his boys, when they came up with us, tended to poke Steve up some, as you poke a damp fire: not too vigorously, but thoroughly. Steve took it well, bagged his climbers and cut his speed. He seemed relieved, though, when the intermittently roaring racers cut the Boecks boys' chaffing. I believe he'd always seen a lot of sense in technology, even if I couldn't.

About eleven we decided to hang it up and get on back. The dogs, tired from this first run of the year, walked along on loose leashes. We all felt that the main event had already occurred. We dawdled around the slough, up the hill and past the straw pile. We scuffed along, Rhiney's boys walking the dogs ahead. The lantern lit the whitish undersides of the apple leaves, and the winding down of the racers just let us catch, for what seemed the hundredth time, an imitation of Steve's desperate, "Get 'em, Tracey!" as he flew from the maple. Then it happened.

It's really not believable. But try, anyway. Tracey pricked up her ears, put down her nose, went "Ho!" and broke for the hen house. Fox and Ranter took off, too, through the rusty yard wire, through the square chicken trapdoor that we'd forgotten to bolt. All three hounds, bellering like sixty, disappeared into the looming hen house. Then a hundred cornish cross chickens began to sail through the rusty mesh windows, big white chickens in full chicken flight, and after them a good-sized mutant coon, fire-red in the lantern light and covered with feathers, and then the baying of the dogs, too close to the ground to make it out the high windows but not about to be forgotten. Of course, I haven't forgotten them.

Steve stayed to help put those hundred chickens away again. Rhiney's boys rolled laughing out of the apple trees that the chickens tried, again, to roost in. Rhiney and I finished the medsun nailing new mesh on the chicken house windows. The hounds, returned after a fruitless, joyful hour pursuing that red coon, quietly stowed away the hot mash and kibble mixture that Rhiney kept them on. After midnight, the racers were still. We drove on home.

And now, twenty years later, I've lost track of Steve, "decent" but "hasty." Rhiney's gone to feed the wild chicory; his boys — one to 'Nam and two to the city. A superhighway has flattened the little oat field hill and filled in the sloughs. But I can still hear, "in between," Tracey's "Hoo-eee!"

Doug McLean *became a writer after age sixty. Before that, he spent much of his time in the outdoors and in the classroom as a teacher. On most days, Doug now can be found in his rural home near Brownsville, writing, painting or planning little adventures, such as a bow-hunt for deer, a walk to search for artifacts, a field trip with a geologist or an afternoon afield with his camera. The accompanying story is one result of his travels and reflects his interest in the Niagara Escarpment. He enjoys sharing what he learns with others, in stories or by chatting with visitors to his country home, a former parsonage.*

The Spear Point

DOUG McLEAN

*In his hand, the spear point seemed almost
to glow as he turned it over and over,
studying its delicate workmanship.
How could anyone, he wondered, make
something like this from a piece of stone?*

The golden retriever, Rusty, looked up expectantly and began to thump his tail on the floor, accurately reading Mark's intention. This time, however, Rusty did not go along; Mark intended to bowhunt for deer by himself. Before getting into his things, he stood a moment at the front window, eyes thoughtfully upon the stretch of ground he planned to walk.

Not far in front of him, the land dropped off in the form of a ninety-foot cliff, know locally as the ledge. He saw its winding, tree-covered course progressing toward Lake Winnebago and knew it arched hundreds of miles above the Great Lakes to where the waters of Niagara Falls plunged over it. He would hunt along the ledge.

He left then, leaving lonesome dog howls far behind, and crossed the lands of rural neighbors, first Berger, then Braford, then Binning and Stafford, good people whom he knew well. Sometimes he wondered what the earlier owners of this land had been like.

Mark passed through a tiny marsh where deer sometimes bedded, and where springs seeped out of limestone bedrock to form a creek that dropped over the limestone in a series of two-foot waterfalls. Perhaps Indians had once camped here. A little farther on, the ledge emerged as a true cliff, and Mark was soon quietly hunting in the woods along the top, his feet crunching too loudly on the leaves, until the sound diminished as he began following a deer trail. Sometimes he stepped to the edge to look for deer below, among the trees and marsh. Eventually, he came to where the ledge began a long loop south, forming a marsh-filled bay a mile wide, before it turned back to the northeast. From here, Mark could survey the entire marsh.

Directly below him was a miniature canyon in the limestone, evidence of the great pressure of glacial ice, which ten thousand years ago had fractured the face of the cliff. This canyon bisected other fractures to make natural intersections and small caves, many of which Mark has explored.

Mark descended, grasping tree roots and other projections, until he was at the canyon bottom. Then he made his way through a passage leading to a natural limestone balcony, from which he could survey the marsh and watch for deer at the spring directly below. Halfway through the passage, he halted as something caught his eye. There, at his feet, contrasting against the black humus, lay a snow-white stone spear point. Realization and delight struck him at once, and he breathed an audible, "Ah!"

In his hand, the point seemed almost to glow as he turned it over and over, studying its delicate workmanship, unlike anything he had seen in local collections. The point was symmetrical and very thin, its graceful sides deeply notched at the rear to form a tail that fanned out like a bird's. Tiny serrations ran along each side.

That evening, Mark sat in his armchair and examined the point again. Rusty lay on the floor beside him, still sighing occasionally at the injustice of having been left at home, but Mark ignored him as he pondered the beauty and craftsmanship in the new-found artifact. How could anyone, he wondered, make something like this from a piece of stone?

———————————— ✐ ————————————

In the year 1250, far to the south, at a site on the Crawfish River that one day would be called Aztalan, Stone Master sat in front of his thatched lodge, a rectangular affair made of sticks plastered with mud. From his comfortable seat of folded buffalo hide, he nodded to a lookout on one of the towers in the stockaded wall that encircled his village.

He examined a slab of snow-white flint the size of a man's hand, from which he intended to make a small ceremonial spear point requested by his chief. The rock was not of poor local chert, nor was it the beautiful honey-colored, sugar-textured material from a place eight days north. Rather, it had traveled hundreds of miles by canoe with Indian traders from the south, men who had preformed it to reduce weight, and dulled its edges to prevent its cutting through the carrying sack.

Conscious of its value, Stone Master struck it sharply with a shaft of deer antler the thickness of a child's wrist. With each expert stroke, a large flake, or spall, fell off the slab. Taking the most ideal piece, he studied it, looking for thick edges that had the proper angles. If necessary, he produced such edges with careful blows from a smaller deer antler billet. Then, carefully controlling the direction, angle and power of his blows, he struck downward at the edges, while holding the piece level in his palm. Each percussion made a long, thin flake fall off on the underside, into his hand. To prevent crushing, sometimes he ground the edges with a stone.

After turning the piece over and performing the same steps on the other side, he laid the antler billet down and picked up a pointed tine of deer antler. Again he prepared edges, and with the tine pressed a series of small flakes off both sides. Stone master smiled. This piece was not dictating the form of the finished piece but was allowing him full control.

Finally, with great care and skill, he used a very sharp deer tine to press out the notches at the tail end. With pride, he stood, dusted the waste flakes off the pad that protected his hand and thigh, licked a tiny flake wound on his left forefinger, and hurried to the lodge of his chief.

———————————— ✿ ————————————

Two Indian experts examined Mark's artifact.
"Late Archaic," said one. "Or possibly Hopewell."

"Middle Mississippian," said the other. "It couldn't be Upper Mississippian; they made only very small arrow points."

They agreed that the material was not local, or even from Wisconsin, and that it probably reached the area through trade.

It would have mattered little to Mark that the second opinion was correct, but it did fire his imagination to think of Indians of diverse cultures traveling long distances to barter peacefully the special goods they owned, by way of skill or geography. He learned from one expert that peace often reigned between western plains tribes and mountain tribes because the plains Indians needed poles from the mountains for their teepees, and mountain Indians needed buffalo skins from the plains for their teepees. He had guessed that Indians journeyed afar only to hunt or make war. Now, he wondered whether an Indian had ever used his spear point against an enemy.

———————————⚬———————————

About four hundred years after Stone Master made the spear point, a Winnebago chief dismissed his breathless nephew, who had trotted a mile to bring him unsettling news. The chief was Tall Oak, and his family's wigwam stood on a knoll between the marsh and the ledge, where it made its southward loop. The nephew had seen an armed intruder from an unknown tribe, but he had not scouted the man long enough to learn more. The other men were away hunting. Tall Oak wanted to kick the reed mat wall of the wigwam, but decided it would not dignify his title to do so. Better, he thought, to consult with the powerful spiritual objects in his medicine bag.

While his wife moved respectfully to the other side of the fire, Tall Oak opened the medicine bag, a richly decorated otter skin complete with head and feet, and poured the dozen objects onto a soft deerskin. Among them were an agate he had found after a battle, a stick with bear claw marks (from the bear whose attack he had escaped), and the snow-white spear point. He recalled the story of his great-great-grandfather's trip south, to trade with strange tribes, bringing back, among other things, the spear point, which by tradition had been passed on to successive sons. The spear point held his attention more than the other objects on the deerskin. He would use its power now.

Selecting a two-foot strip of deer sinew, he separated a narrow strip of fibers, then soaked it in water to soften it. Next, he lashed the sinew around the notched shaft of an arrow, then around the point itself. Finally, he held the shaft over the fire to make the sinew dry and tight. All that remained was to melt some crystallized hide glue over the fire and daub it on, to make a rock-hard binding. This he asked his wife to do while he finished his preparations.

His moccasins made little sound on the footpath that followed the curving ledge. When he came to the stream that tumbled down its limestone stairway, he heard not only the gurgling falls but the heavier splash of a beaver in the pond. Approaching softly, he looked out of the foliage and saw the stranger standing in the pond, spear raised, gazing at the water. Three more steps put Tall Oak in the open only ten yards from the man, who looked up suddenly.

In the first instant, alien eyes locked together and faces remained frozen. In the second instant, Tall Oak's arm drew and held the bowstring, while the stranger's raised and cocked the spear. Then time dragged. High overhead, a string of geese conversed musically, unheard by the men below. Tall Oak dared not put down his bow to use sign language, so he blurted out, "Why are you here?"

"Beaver," came the reply in his own tongue.

"Who are you?"

"Snowshoe, of the Fox people."

"How do you speak my tongue?"

"I have been among your people to the north for a year."

Each noticed the other slowly lowering his weapon. More questions and more answers, with some sign language, revealed that the Foxes had been pushed west over the large lake of the Hurons, the larger lake Gitchee Gumee, and Lake Michigan, by the Iroquois. Snowshoe explained that his tribe lacked some skills needed in this new land and had learned to catch beaver for their fur, to trade with white men, also pushing west. Tall Oak, too, wanted to know how to catch many beaver.

One reason Tall Oak was chief was that his vision often leaped ahead, and now, in the Fox's story, he could feel the uncertain winds of change. He invited the man home for more talk. In the end, the Winnebagoes let the Fox band trap beaver through the winter in exchange for lessons. Tall Oak gave the white spear point to Snowshoe, in return for an equally symbolic gift of friendship, a pipe carved from a soft red stone found only in a land far to the north and west. Snowshoe also gave the Winnebagoes a supply of castor oil, a secretion from beaver glands, used to bait the traps.

On a sunny February day, Mark's six-year-old granddaughter took the spear point from its resting place on the window sill. Holding it up to the sunlight so that its thin edges showed a halo of translucence, she asked, "Grandad, can I play with this?"

"You can hold it for a while, but it is not a toy."

"I bet Indian children played with it, Grandad."

"No, it was probably used for hunting deer."

Neither knew that, in fact, they were both correct.

On another bright February day two hundred years earlier, a Fox Indian prepared to leave the smoky warmth of his bark-covered wigwam to go hunting. The lodges of his people were below the sheltering rim of the ledge. For a time the Winnebagoes had been here, but they had long since been forced west.

It had been a hard winter for White Hare's lodge. Most of the grains, nuts and dried berries were gone. There had been no meat for ten days. He had lost arrows in the snow, one after another, missing the only game in sight — small creatures like squirrels and rabbits. Now he did not need a quiver. There was only one arrow, tipped with a slightly-too-large white ceremonial spear point, which he used only because there was nothing else.

The snow squeaked under his high-cut, rabbit-fur-lined moccasins until he reached the soft, deeper snow of the marsh. By the time he crossed over snow and ice to the clumps of willow, he was becoming cold, but the cold helped him go farther into the marsh that day, for it had firmed up the ice. It was more good fortune that made a deer jump from its bed, only to meet the instant arrow from White Hare's bow.

As the deer fled, the arrow's feathered shaft bobbed in the sunlight. Flying water droplets sparkled as the deer broke through thin ice and plunged on. The deer was soon out of reach beyond bunches of willows, and White Hare knew he must brave the cold water if his family was to avoid hunger.

Breaking at last out of the willows and the icy, black water, White Hare saw the deer far ahead, about to leave the marsh and reach the western curve of the ledge. When he had covered half the distance, White Hare forgot his painful, ice-encrusted lower legs for a moment as he watched the deer sink to its knees. As he approached, the deer rose again and tried to clamber up a mass of tumbled boulders. White Hare found it there.

Working with haste to save his feet, he soon had the gutted deer over his shoulder and was concentrating on the warmth of his lodge only twenty minutes away. The small spear point, still attached to the arrow shaft, lay lost under the trampled, bloody snow high up in the rock fall.

Some years later, in 1832, just above the spot where the deer fell, an encampment of Indians was concealed in a narrow canyon in the face of the ledge. In the outer canyon wall, a narrow passage led to a natural stone balcony, where a young brave intently studied the far rim of the ledge as it bent north and east.

Above him towered broken sections of cliff. On top of one such block, soft green grass grew in the sunlight, and on this bright little island a small Indian girl played with a beautiful white spear point she had found among the rocks below. The lookout tilted his head back to look up at her smiling face. He noted the spear point and was glad she now had time to play after many days of travel and hardship.

She spoke then to an elderly chief who entered the rocky passage. "Grandfather Blackhawk! See what I have found!"

While the soft, mellow tones of the elderly voice mixed with the musical chirpings of the child, the lookout turned back to search the far curve of the ledge. He tensed at what he saw: glints of metal in the late afternoon sun, wisps of smoke from several campfires. There was no doubt what this foreshadowed, and he turned quickly to Blackhawk.

"The soldiers are coming."

Ever since Blackhawk had led his band of Sacs north from their homeland on the Rock River in Illinois Territory, the white militia had kept on their trail, under orders of the Illinois governor. The trail of the Sacs meandered north into the lands of the Foxes and Winnebagoes. Several times they thought they were being left alone, but the pursuit had continued. Now they fled again. This time they would go west to the river Ouisconsing, cross it, and continue to the big river, Misses Sepe. Perhaps, on the other side, in the lands of the Sioux, there would be rest and safety.

The tall island of limestone remained undisturbed for many years. Each spring, wispy green grass grew in the shallow soil, and nestled in that grass was the white spear point. Here it remained while the earth made the long passage around the sun another one hundred and fifty times. Then, one moonlit night in March, a pair of red foxes engaged in a courtship dance dashed to the top of the limestone island. Their brief cavorting dislodged the spear point, which fell fifteen feet into the passageway below.

A few years after his discovery, Mark stood with his bow at the edge of the marsh, resting from his long walk. He was here because of temptation. He had learned that the spear point met the legal requirements for modern broadheads and that its weight was good, and so, with thirty-pound fishline and epoxy, he secured the point to one of his old cedar shafts. Balancing the arrow on his finger, he found it to be ideal, and himself clever. So, he went to the marsh to shoot a deer the way the Indians did, leaving his compound bow at home in favor of an old wood and fiberglass recurve.

Mark stood where a farm field sloped to meet the tall marsh grass. The warm breeze blew in off the marsh, wafting down bits of cattail and carrying the essence of marsh hay and steamy bog. It was too much a bluebird day, and in Mark's mind, napping competed strongly with marsh slogging.

Twenty yards out in the marsh, a deer had just concluded its own nap. When it slowly rose, its antlers appeared to Mark as no more than dry branches, but the truth registered as the majestic head and massive body also came smoothly up. The movement transpired so casually that Mark half expected the buck to stretch and yawn.

Then the deer was standing broadside, its large brown eyes seeming to regard Mark as of little consequence. Mark slowly raised the bow and smoothly drew the arrow. Then he held, as the buck's gaze shifted and seemed to fasten on the snow-white spear point, as though its brightness were a visual magnet.

Mark needed only a second to calm his racing heart. A message came from one corner of his brain: Release! Instead, he froze. The buck whirled and took the first great leap. Antlers bouncing away held Mark's gaze until they blended with tangled willow. He lowered his bow shakily.

Trudging up the ledge, Mark wondered, "Why did I hold back?" An upside down chickadee peered at him, but had no answer. "Well, at least I didn't lose the arrow," he said to the departing bird. And suddenly he knew.

At sunset, Mark stood at the window, watching the last rays highlight the far west-facing rim of the ledge and the farms upon it, the foreground already in shadow. As the sky darkened, the rim became outlined by the lights of farms and homes, each light marking the home of a family, not so different from the families of Indians whose campfires and signal fires may once have traced the curving ledge.

Out there in that fading landscape, a courageous people had truly existed, had walked among majestic oaks, had drunk from sparkling streams. Under the sheltering cliffs they braved the fierce weather and learned the skills of survival. Amid the land's bounty they spoke their soft language to the spirits, loved their children, and treasured things of beauty. Mark gazed out upon those ancient grounds, then down upon the spear point in his palm. Slowly, reverently, he closed his fingers around it.

R. Chris Halla, *of Appleton, is a poet and writer with roots "so deep in the Wisconsin landscape that they poke out the other side." He grew up in a little river town in the middle of the state and has since lived or spent "quality time" in every other part of Wisconsin. Chris is an avid fly fisher, upland bird hunter, camper and all-around river rat. His poetry and nonfiction can be found regularly in the literary, outdoors and general interest press. His latest poetry chapbook is* Water, *published by Wolfsong of Sturtevant, Wis. His fly fishing book,* Everyone's Illustrated Guide to Trout on a Fly, *came out last year from Frank Amato Publishing. He is an award-winning video producer, a DNR-certified fishing instructor, a literacy tutor, and an amateur gourmet game, chili and barbecue cook. His favorite fishing partner is his wife, Janet.*

Nutting Maxwell Road

R .   C H R I S   H A L L A

---

*Perfect timing is to arrive early enough
to find a few nuts just fallen, to hear
others falling. There is, you tell yourself
at this time, no sin in coaxing from
the trees clusters of nuts that are
about to fall anyway.*

I am alone in my car, pulled off onto the
wide grass shoulder, surveying what I can
make out from here of the length of Maxwell
Road. There may be no other single place where
my past, my present and my future connect as they
do here.

Maxwell Road is 1.7 arrow-straight miles long, just wide
enough for two cars to meet and pass without touching. There
are four farms, one with an apple orchard. There are four dogs,
one yellow and three black. The road runs east-west, its southern side edged by a row of shagbark hickories, thick with brush
that grows thicker every year. There's asparagus off the northern roadside, plus a couple of stunted plum trees with tangled
branches, one apple tree that still produces fruit every other
year, though it hasn't grown in a decade, and a half-dozen stray
hickories that appear to have wandered across to avoid crowd-
ing on the other side.

Only a few wildflowers grow along Maxwell Road. Clover,
of course. Goldenrod, chicory, sunflowers, chickweed, black-
eyed Susans. The most spectacular of all is the bloom of the
shagbark hickory with its enlarged bud scales. The rusty
orange flower appears only briefly in spring. Many have never

seen the flower, because they are afield only at harvest time. Some who have never seen it say it doesn't exist, that it is as elusive as the Raintree. Its shape suggests it might be called the shagbark orchid. The strange and beautiful flower is a regal, if fleeting, foreteller of the trees' harvest a few months later. During the last days of inland trout season, about a month before the gunpowder days of October, the hickory nuts ripen and fall along Maxwell Road. Their husks soon begin to turn from green to brown. Eventually they become black, staining the shell and the meat, tainting the flavor.

If you have watched the shagbark's progress from mid-May to September, you will be able to be on Maxwell Road as the ripe nuts drop softly into the tall grass of the ditches or bounce on the road's hard, gray surface. Perfect timing is to arrive early enough to find a few nuts just fallen, to hear others falling. There is, you tell yourself at this time, no sin in coaxing from the trees clusters of nuts that are about to fall anyway.

The greatest reward for monitoring the grove daily from the first week of September comes the morning you are able to start picking ahead of everyone and everything. With each passing day thereafter, the ground becomes littered with hundreds, then, quickly, thousands of drilled and emptied tan nut skeletons that mark where the squirrels have been, but you have not.

When I began nutting Maxwell Road, squirrels were the only competition. The road was a well-kept secret with its farmers and, as far as I could tell, almost no one else. The farmers had little interest in the hickories along the road. There were enough trees in their yards and fields to keep them well supplied with nuts.

It's too long ago now to remember how old I was when the ritual of nutting Maxwell Road started for me. I would have been very young. Four. Maybe five. The dark green 1950 Chevrolet Deluxe sedan would have been parked off to the side as far as possible without being in the ditch, facing east at the road's far western end.

I would have been with my mother and Aunt Curly, both wearing men's plaid shirts and baggy cotton pants with narrow western belts. Some things are certain. Even today, when I see someone wearing a western belt with one of those small, silver, horseshoe-shaped buckles, I see the one on the belt my mother always wore. Then I see her in a spring woods picking wild-flowers, or making camp next to a trout stream, or nutting on Maxwell Road.

My first nutting experiences seem small, insignificant, but they left a powerful imprint that often brought me back to the road. As a child exploring the countryside outside our small town, I came with friends to study birds and bugs and flowers; to play tag, cowboy and soldier. During the summer months of my teens, Maxwell Road was one of those rare places where you could park in peace with your girlfriend, free from the disturbing presence of dateless buddies.

Maxwell Road offered a young hunter opportunities for both pheasants and Hungarian partridge. The age of fencerows and unmowed ditches was coming to an end. With them, the days of plentiful wild pheasants in Winnebago County would pass, too. In the late Fifties and early Sixties, however, there were still birds everywhere there was corn or long grass.

Pheasant season is a month away. I have come to scout, to see what kind of sign I can find that will help me fill my vest on opening day. Virtually all the property along Maxwell Road is private. Fortunately the farmers who own these fields of corn, soybeans and wheat don't mind a few local kids with shotguns who harmlessly wander their land.

I walk well into the cornfield, maybe a hundred rows in. Then I hike up and down every fifth row or so, working my way back toward the road, to see if I might put up birds now that could provide shooting a month hence.

After the last corn row, I zigzag through the grass between the corn and the roadside hickories. It's a poor day when this fence row doesn't yield a bird or two. First a hen goes up, then another. A big rooster panics and flushes from beneath the wide-reaching hickory branches with the commotion only a cock pheasant can raise. I shoulder my imaginary gun. "Bang." It is, of course, a perfect shot. He glides into the corn unharmed.

On the walk along the road, back to the car three-quarters of a mile away, I absent-mindedly inspect the ditch, bending often to fill my pockets with nuts that must have just started falling a day or two earlier. By the time I get back to the car, I wish I would have had the foresight to grab a grocery bag before leaving home.

———————————

I took my wife nutting on Maxwell Road a month after we married. A few years later, we nutted Maxwell Road with my mother the day before our son was born. Both he and our daughter, who arrived on a winter morning five years later, always looked forward to the annual nutting excursions: Brown grocery bags in hand, at first picking up the nuts, hulls and all, along with woolly-bear caterpillars, interesting stones, bird feathers and acorn caps. I don't think they cared what became of the nuts after picking. Wild rice and hickory nut stuffing, cranberry-hickory nut bread, the quart jar of nut-meats, all were far removed from kids having fun on a country road.

———————————

It's a cool, sunny day, September 1986. We've come nutting in our new car with sliding doors on both sides. We all agree this is the perfect car for nutting. Josh is eleven. Rachel is six. Josh goes with his mother to the first of the hickories on the south side of the road. Rachel goes with me, up a ways to the first trees on the north side — the sunny side — of the road. We start on the road's west end and work east, as we did when I first came nutting here with my mother.

We talk about the size of the nuts and the height of the grass around the trees where Rachel feels along with her sneak-ered feet for the telltale, stone-like bumps. When one pokes against her foot, she goes down into the grass to pick it up. She is interested in the kinds of bugs that live in this grass and whether there are any on her. She also wonders about the grass snakes we sometimes see here. When the ground yields few nuts, she asks if I will lift her up so she can pick some off the tree. I explain, of course, that it's better not to do that. Then, having made the required disclaimer, I lift her up to pick a few. Some of them fall at our lightest touch.

Rachel wonders if we have more nuts than Josh and Mom. I empty my bag into hers. I can hear Josh and his mother talking down the road where they are almost hidden in the brushy ditch and tree shadows. Most likely he's asking if they have more nuts than Rachel and Dad. They combine the contents of their bags, too.

When we meet back at the car, we're all happy that so far none of us have gathered more than the others. The contents of both bags are mostly tan, only a hint of green husk here and there. Both children learned early on that it's easier to pop off the husks when you first pick the nuts than it is to get them off later. While they take no part and show no interest in the extended ritual of soaking, drying, cracking, canning, they know the more immediate obligations of a person who picks up a nut and puts it in a bag.

Somehow Maxwell Road has been spared the widening and other "improvements" that have destroyed the character of so many rural passageways. This country road is a constant when everything else has changed, and life has sometimes been unkind. During eleven years while we lived far from Maxwell Road, we still made annual trips back for nutting. Now we find ourselves again living a short half-hour away. My office is only five minutes away. Daily crop checks as summer turns to autumn are easy. The last couple of years, I've driven out to Maxwell Road mostly for memories, most vivid when the trees are weighted down with clusters of green nuts almost, but not quite, ready to fall.

There, in the distance, is a little boy picking nuts with his mother. Closer in there's a teenager kicking along the fence row for pheasants. As he fades away, a young man appears with his family, all happily filling brown paper bags from the roadside ditches. Finally, there is a middle-aged man alone inside his car, looking out, not sure whether the vision is clearer through the windshield or the rearview mirror.

Justin Isherwood

Tha mi tuanthanach is Gaelic for "I am farmer." That is how Justin defines himself. Justin, son Isaac and brother Gary farm nine hundred acres of sandy loam near Plover. Daughter Heather is a weekly newspaper editor in Milwaukee, "though she is obligated to donate the nurture and training of any offspring to the farm," her father says. "Lynn, my wife of thirty years, is a West Allis girl I lured to the farm under false pretenses, something about temporary." The farm produces potatoes, snap beans and corn, along with batches of maple syrup, blackberries, and wild grape and dandelion wine "to heal what the price per bushel won't or can't." Justin devotes winters to writing and is widely published in regional and national outlets. His Book of Plough, a collection of essays about the joys, sorrows and humor of family farm life, was published in 1995.

They Wore Plaid

JUSTIN ISHERWOOD

*The deputy sheriff had supper at
his cousin's farm on many occasions,
where the missus served up a crock
of stew so hearty it still had a pulse,
at the center of this stew a lean loin of
untraveled venison, fried a few minutes
beforehand in a cast-iron skillet with
butter, onion, worcestershire and
a touch of single-malt tartan hooch.*

A neighbor, now deceased and out of range of the warden, did not believe in his lifetime that farmers should have to purchase a deer-hunting license. He felt this motivation to a heightened degree of attachment, despite it might appear counterproductive of venison. Which is bad enough as far as law-abiding behavior is concerned. It gets worse.

This neighbor was also of the opinion that hunting deer at the far end of November was an absolute counterbalance to how venison is supposed to taste. The animal at this juncture is so doped up with sexual excess as to chase a female, of any sort, any age, any education, any family; as a result, not at all an edible beast. This, the same creature who had spent the preceding month at ninety-four percent of terminal velocity, hadn't had a good night's sleep, was anxious the entire time, pent-up with jealousies it could not reason with, tortured by eroticisms that wouldn't quit and wasn't eating a balanced diet neither. This animal the agency advertised as the one my neighbor ought to hunt.

Hunt, they said, in the far back corner of November, which pretty much coincides with the solar phase that in the Northern Hemisphere borders on the egregious. In all likelihood several notches worse than egregious. In other words, a cold-weather hunt. Mitten weather, frostbite season, this the hunt allocated indiscriminately on farmer and villager alike. Whether or not you plant corn or alfalfa or clover, whether or not you leave a woods in the middle of what every other business-minded person thinks is perfectly developable. When all hunters pay the same price for the same inedible roasts and chops, in weather like than not a lot better for putting up firewood than hunting.

As a result of his conscience, my neighbor poached. He did so for most of fifty years without getting caught, though it was a close thing once or twice. Once his brother-in-law ratted on him and told the deputy, who was a cousin to both, which is how neighborly folk at the back end of the sandburr frontier were. Told the deputy straight out that Harold was poaching deer out of season, without a license, which really didn't matter since it was already out of season. Also at night, also illegal; using bait, another violation; with a small caliber and a silencer — while wearing plaid. About 3,648 years in the state penitentiary if the statutes were unrolled full length.

The deputy sheriff of course knew this already, having had supper at his cousin's farm on many occasions, where the missus served up a crock of stew so hearty it still had a pulse, a stew as few are now capable, which included new-ground rutabagas that had a flavor even rarer and more exquisite than truffles. To this were added black moor carrots, onions, taters and a hatful of butter mushrooms by way of Mrs. Soik, who picked them by the bushel and canned them in gallon containers for neighbors who saw to it that her road was plowed in winter, being she was a widow. Her woodshed was filled, her outlets rewired, the excess kittens drowned, all for the favor of a gallon of mushrooms as only a Polish Catholic lady can pick them, guided by the Virgin Mother, and not once poisonous.

At the center of this stew, a lean loin of untraveled venison, sliced across the grain, fried a few minutes beforehand in a cast-iron skillet with butter, onion, worcestershire and a touch, just a touch, of single-malt tartan hooch. This for that taste o' the peat you can only otherwise get if you drag the beast across the marsh a couple of miles after a hard rain, but easier and more hygienic from a bottle. Served with fresh bread and cold butter. The deputy of course could no more turn in my neighbor for poaching than he could turn himself inside out by hanging onto his adenoids.

Fifty years my neighbor poached a specimen at the salt lick on a night in October with a .22 caliber single-shot rifle from inside the corncrib, using a spotlight connected to a six-volt car battery.

The second time he was almost caught was by Frank Hornsby, the warden who hated poaching about as much as a mortal man can hate anything, who had been told repeatedly by villagers that there was this farmer down on the edge of the big empty that poached every year, and wasn't it about time to make an example of him? Which causes a problem for law enforcement, being the law is evident enough, but so are the man's wood lots when his neighbors are clearing out woods fast as a twenty-ton Cat can do the business, not even saving the saw logs, all of it going up in smoke. When Frank knew very well clearing out woods right down past the trilliums wasn't considered poaching.

What Frank Hornsby did was visit the junkyard of the Dombroski Brothers up on County Y, who had the part of any car made in the Free World since 1941. He bought from them the rusty bumper off a 1960 VW Beetle, this before the Wolfsburg plant started getting fancy with oblongs and umlauts. Plain VW bumper is what the warden wanted. Wrapped in brown paper and delivered to Harold along with a sermon on illegality that ran fourteen or fifteen seconds, the latter portion of which was more about trout, ditching and wet flies.

When Harold Edwards, who will remain nameless for sake of anonymity, asked what was the thing wrapped in the brown paper, Frank Hornsby went solemn. He scratched himself in a scholarly fashion, then a diplomatic fashion, finally in a theological fashion. Searching, as we all can sympathize, for the perfect metaphor. Hornsby to this point had made something like 65,000 arrests for poaching alone, some for trout and quite a few for prairie chicken, also grouse, red-headed wood-peckers and badgers; mostly, however, his guardianship had been slanted toward the white-tailed kangaroo. And the patent vision that one day this same herbivore would be numerous and seen from every porch and barn door. Metaphors in this situation are exacting. One false step and they might both spend six hundred years in the state peniten-tiary. The gospel writers had no greater task of adjudicating the woes and hopes of human beings with vernacular utter-ances than what Frank Hornsby had to come up with at this moment. A haiku won't do, ancient Sanskrit neither; it all came down to a word, a single revelatory word.

"Roadkill" is what Frank said. What was in the brown paper? Roadkill.

So it happened at Betty's Roundhouse Cafe, named for the curve in the road, in the days that followed that a patron, who shall also remain nameless, talked over-loud about folks getting away with murder right under the nose of mister official war-den. Poaching is what they meant. How everyone knew that at this very moment, hanging in Harold's corncrib was his cut of the local herd. And it only October 12.

Frank knew as Marshal Dillon knew, high noon had arrived at Betty's Cafe. Well, Mister Banker, how about you and I go visit this alleged corncrib? I'll drive the car, you run the siren. Which sounded pretty good to a man whose biggest noise on any average day was the ratchet crank of an adding machine.

They arrived soon after at Harold's farm. He wasn't at the house, so they followed the tractor road behind the barn, dodg-ing as it did one of the nicest and squattest raccoon oaks you'll ever chance to see. On which the banker observed out loud that Harold could have a nice straight road if he just got rid of that one tree. Frank only nodded.

Frank asked the financier, feeling close now to the warden what with the mutual pursuit of a crime, have you noticed the nice set of center-pivots the Wycoshes set up outside of town? Booming thing this center-pivot stuff; booming I tell you. If you want, I could get you in on a little investment thing we got going; it'll pay off a lot more than standard interest. It's risky, of course, but only a little.

Frank motioned with his head as they were approaching Harold's corncrib, set at the edge of the woods, which a decent corncrib oughtn't do if you didn't want coons and flying squirrels to pilfer the crop before it served a more agricultural purpose. Inside the slat walls they could make out the hanging carcass of a deer.

Ah ha, caught red-handed, gleed the banker. Didn't I tell you, Frank, didn't I tell you?

Frank only frowned and walked up to the corncrib door. The banker enthusiastically turned the handle and looked in.

I was gonna do that with a stick.

What?

I was gonna do the handle with a stick. Prints you know, fingerprints, prima facie; now that handle has your prints on it.

John D. the banker deflated about six hundred cubic meters, when only moments before he felt like a righteous posse in hot pursuit.

Gawd dammit, don't touch anything else, Frank instructed as they advanced into the gloom. Fishing from his pocket an enormous six-cell flashlight quite capable of giving a suntan, he rested the beam on a field-dressed doe weighing about a hundred and three pounds.

There's your case warden, sang the banker, running his hand enthusiastically through a sleek sheen of black hair that looked like bulrushes blown flat. The man smelled of fresh aftershave and it past 2:30 in the afternoon. So, you gonna make an arrest?

Nope.

No? Frank, Frank, you gotta ... he's been poaching since he was twelve years old. When my father ran the bank he'd plan a visit to the Edwards place at noon 'cause of Mrs. Edwards' biscuits.

Bread.

Oh yah, I guess it was bread, not biscuits; and how they always had venison stew, least he thought it was venison. Myself I don't care for venison, too gamey, you know? Warden, you gotta make an arrest, there's evidence enough here to convict the Pope.

John, you missed a detail … Frank turned his flashlight on the forequarter of the deer where a patch of hide was missing, and in its place rusty bits of chrome.

Roadkill.

Frank, Frank, isn't even having any deer illegal?

Technically that's true. Harold should have gotten a carcass release by the sheriff's department, but I'm not going to get involved with people who pick up roadkills, otherwise I'll end up doing it myself and the fewer times I go to the deer dump the better. Say, John, have you ever been there? How about you and I drive up? It's just a little ways in the moraine. You might see a nice rack for your office.

Really?

I'll saw it off for you but the smell gets to my stomach, though I know I ought to be used to it by now.

Thanks, Frank, I think I'll pass. Besides, I've got a mountain goat from my Alaska trip. Best shot I ever made. Weatherby, you know, .303 heavy grain, must have been three-fifty, four hundred yards. The thing skidded down under a glacier, and it took all three guides to haul it out.

Like to see it sometime, Frank said.

You do that, the banker gushed as he opened the passenger's door. They drove back to the Roundhouse Cafe, talking a little more about Alaska, and John recounting his trip to the Bitterroot for the best trout fishing he had ever seen.

Little rich for me, John, I'm afraid.

They parted in the parking lot, Frank waving again as John unlocked his newly washed car. Frank felt an irrational need to take the long muddy road across the marsh, to cure what only a long muddy road going nowhere can cure. Frank Hornsby, it is said, always wore plaid.

Jay Reed was born to a family of commercial fishermen and professional trappers, and learned early in life the value, and joy, of owning skilled, well-trained hunting dogs. His late brother, a life-long bachelor, was fond of saying that every man, in his life, is entitled to "at least one good woman and one good dog, not necessarily in that order." An outdoor writer for three decades at the old Milwaukee Journal and now the Journal Sentinel, Jay has hunted and fished in Canada, Cuba, South America, Mexico and in nearly every one of the United States. In 1966 and 1967, he covered the war in Vietnam for his newspaper. Twenty years later, he returned to that country to do another series of stories and to revisit the combat zones. Twice a Pulitzer Prize finalist, Jay has been widely honored for his work in Wisconsin and the Midwest. He lives near the north shore of Lake Michigan with his wife, Christine, and two yellow Labradors, Belle and Maggie.

Thor

JAY REED

*These sights do not come that often
in a lifetime. You see them, early on,
but you don't really appreciate them.
You have to grow old. You have to get
close to death to see sunsets and
wild, free ducks as they really are.*

*I*f I could look back over my life and select just one day and be able to make it last forever, I know which one it would be. Easy choice. A no-brainer, as they say.

It would be that late October day, deep in the swamps of the Chippewa River, the wind curling and snapping out of the northeast, the temperature dropping, when my old dog told me he was going to die soon.

Thor was in his twelfth year that fall. Already a living legend, arguably the best-known hunting dog in the Midwest, he displayed the wear and tear of the miles that had gone before. But his eyes were bright and his heart was strong and the desire that drove him through the stubble fields of Saskatchewan, to the prairies of South Dakota, to the flooded low country of Mexico, to every crook and corner of Wisconsin and Iowa and Nebraska still burned within.

The yellow Labrador had been the subject of countless newspaper and magazine stories over the years. He had hunted for, and with, some of the biggest names in the conservation field. And most of those people remember him to this day as the best duck dog they ever saw. But I knew it would be that way, or had a hunch, at least, when he was eight months old.

He weighed about seventy pounds then, and he had grown gangly, leggy. But his chest was deep and his back was straight and his flanks rippled with hardening muscle. And he loved to train. He was not only willing to make one more retrieve, go through one more exercise. He wanted to.

The proof of anything is in performance, right? At that young age, Thor demonstrated extraordinary ability before a hundred or so spectators at a dog-training seminar. He was flawless. He made two long, spectacular water retrieves through the toughest swamp cover, drawing applause from those who watched and easily out-hunting two other retrievers three times his age.

Back then, Thor's biggest problem was his inability to stand by and watch other retrievers work. He was over-eager. He wanted to make every retrieve. He wanted to do every exercise. He was not a "gentleman on line," as they said in field train-ing. And, every so often, he tried to cheat on his retrieves. He'd stray off line. But he could mark a downed bird like a champi-on. And he was steady to shot from the beginning.

And he learned. There were those who said Thor should have been good. He had the blood for it. His sire, Candlewood's Nifty Nick, was a Wisconsin open field trial champion and one of the state's most celebrated stud dogs. Thor looked like Nifty Nick, hunted like him, behaved like him, and displayed many of the dog's most significant traits. I thought about all that, and more, that day in the Chippewa River marshes. I knew that Thor was getting on toward the end of the line, but I never allowed myself to think that he would one day die. And it remains painful for me to recall all of that, even now that the snows of two winters have fallen upon his grave. It hurts me to think about it, like having the same tooth filled three times in one day. So consider the recounting of it all here as a sort of therapy for an old man who still sees the ghost of his dog every day and in his trou-bled dreams at night.

This is how it was that day in October when Thor told me he was about to die. We are at our hunting camp in West-Central Wisconsin, a place of paradise where laughter is para-mount and tears are few.

There is happiness: An old dog courses the swamps and finds the fountain of youth there. He becomes, as he once was, a pup, and he works the water and the wind and the cover and the birds with style and grace and uncommon dignity.

And there is sadness: The old dog has been fed and he has slept and now it is morning and I have to lift him off the couch where he spent the night because his muscles have tightened and his feet are sore and he is old, with only heart and wanting left to pump the engine. The fountain of youth was false.

Or was it?

With each step after that he loosens up, and when he sees me put the shotgun into the truck, his eyes glisten and his tail wags. He is ready. He wants to go. He will go. Which is why I want to cry, because I know time is running out for the dog, and so the hot tears roll down my cheek on a frosty dawn when only the stars can see.

Then I lift him into the truck, an assist that his eyes and gentle growl tell me he does not want. But I do it, and he accepts it because we both know this is how it has to be. And then I drive to the hunting grounds, and the old dog tries to stand in the back of the truck, but he can't because his legs won't let him. So he sits, growling softly, his heart telling him that these are the good times, the best of times.

Maybe he knows his days are numbered. Maybe he knows that there are not that many more retrieves for him to make. Maybe he knows that for him, one day soon, the sunset will write a final chapter to this business called duck hunting, this business called life. Maybe he knows all of that. But I do not. Yet.

He jumps, unaided, to the ground when we reach the boat landing. He is loosening up now. When the boat is in the water, he steps into it without problem, stationing himself, as he has done for a lifetime, close to the stern where I can scratch his ears as we travel into the swamps.

We run for an hour through some of the most beautiful marshland God ever created. Thor knows every inch of it. He has worked it all. He puts his nose into the wind and inhales it deeply. The wind is a river of language to the old dog. He reads it the way the rest of us read books. It is a blue domain, designed only for him.

We reach our pothole of choice. Shouldering the shotgun, a bag of decoys and a pack with lunch, I lead the twenty-minute walk to the place where we have this little blind. There is a bucket for me to sit on. And there is a dry patch of canvas, plus a blanket, upon which Thor can either sit or stand out of the water while we wait for the ducks to come. And they do. But we are selective. There is no need to hurry. We have all day. So take only the best, I tell myself. Let it all last. Let it all linger.

But a mallard drake works the decoys. It swings once and then comes in, wings set. An artist should capture it. I pull on the bird, squeeze the trigger, and it drops into a combination stand of tall marsh grass and buck brush. Thor marks the spot and, on command, goes to fetch.

He works it exactly right and, finally, he emerges from the heavy cover holding the mallard in classic breast grip. The dog comes straight to hand, duck held high out of the water. He comes to me, walks around to my side and sits, offering me the result of all we have worked for, all we have trained for, all we have bragged about and publicly demonstrated over the years. If there is such a thing in this world as a perfect retrieve, this was it.

I take the bird and pat the dog on his heaving sides and tell him that it was good work. He shakes himself, swamp water spraying like a crystal fan, and he smiles. I swear to God, he smiles. And then he takes to scanning the horizon again, as he has done all his life, looking for that which makes his heart pound and his throat fill with a soft growl.

At noon we share a sandwich, Thor and I. He wolfs his share down as he has always done. I eat half of mine and offer him the remaining half. He takes it, giving me a look of gratitude. Or maybe he thinks I'm a dummy, willing to give up such good stuff. Given his age, Thor does not sit and wait for ducks as patiently as when he was younger. So when I let some widgeons and two wood duck hens go by without firing, he snarls at me and pushes at my leg. I forget now what time it was. Late afternoon, I'd guess.

A flock of seven mallards work our decoys. On the second swing I pick a greenhead and drop it. Thor marks the fall. And, on command, he courses out into the open water and on to the gray buck brush, where he finds the bird and picks it up. And this is where it all happens.

Thor picks up the bird, but instead of coming straight back to me, he heads for the far side of the pothole. Instead of coming directly back to me as he had been trained to do, as he had done countless times over the years, he detours across the lumpy weed growth to a strip of high land. I can see him all the way. And he can see me. But the whole operation takes minutes longer than it should. Finally, he comes to heel, bird in mouth, and I take it from him, but there is no praise.

Why did he take the long route? Was he perhaps squeezing one more moment of ecstasy out of a time that for him was rapidly diminishing? I didn't know anything about all that at the time.

We have our limit of ducks for the day, the two mallards and a wood duck that dropped close to us for an easy retrieve. There is nothing left for the two of us to do except watch the movement of birds and take pleasure from it. The dog stands out at the edge of the marsh grass, belly deep in water. He stares across the water and he watches the birds and his tail wags and his eyes glisten and his body trembles.

He is wet and he is muddy, and he shivers along the length of his back and into his flanks. The sun is dropping and darkness is about to cover the swamps and we have to get back to the boat because there is yet a long way to go to camp.

I call to Thor. But he does not respond. He stands out in the water looking and watching and shivering and wondering why I do not shoot. So I walk up to my dog on this evening of evenings and I kneel beside him in the water and watch what he is watching. And in that first moment I know what this is all about.

We see ducks working the skyline, circling, talking and coming in to those places of refuge where they can rest and eat. Beautiful birds. They are the lumber from which eternity is constructed. My dog knows that. And now, I know it.

Thor, I discover then, as if I didn't know it before, is smarter than I am. These sights do not come that often in a lifetime. You see them, early on, but you don't really appreciate them.

You have to grow old. You have to get close to death to see sunsets and wild, free ducks as they really are.

That is why my dog did not respond to call, I am sure now. He was taking one more look. He was sipping from the cup one more time. He was telling me, you see, that he was going to die, that he would never have this opportunity again, and he was making the most of it.

And he was right.

I know all about that now, but I was not capable of putting it all together at the time.

We get back to the boat and he jumps in. We get back to the truck and he jumps in. We get back to camp. After he eats I have to lift him up onto the couch where he will spend the night. I will lift him down in the morning.

If you own an old dog and if you work with him and play with him and live with him and forgive him his shortcomings and beg more time for him, you will understand why I wept that night in duck camp. Thor and I did not hunt together again after that. Some good people salted a field with ringnecks for Thor in December, and we worked them. But it was over. He knew it, and I knew it.

So it came to pass that in July of that next year, Thor went down at thirteen years of age and more miles than you can count. In the end, it makes no difference what anybody else thought about Thor. I knew he was the beginning and the end of everything. I like to believe he thought the same about me.

So give me a day that I can make last forever. No question. Make mine with Thor.

God, how I loved that dog.

Clarence A. Schoenfeld *(1918-96) was a professor of journalism and mass communications at the University of Wisconsin–Madison from 1953-85. He was founding chair of the university's Center for Environmental Studies and founded the Conservation Commu-nications program in the late 1960s. He was also a prolific writer, producing articles for outdoor and nature magazines as well as numerous books and texts on environmental affairs, university administration and journalism. His column "Outofdoors" appeared for many years in the Madison newspapers. His books include the classic* Down Wisconsin Sideroads, *published in 1979.*

Memo About Mallards

CLAY SCHOENFELD

*For one awesome second there is
nothing in time but you, a little stretch
of windswept pothole, and a huddle of
wild waterfowl. For a magic moment,
you look right into the eye of nature.
The memory is forever.*

When a hunter reaches his mid-70s, his days afield are numbered. But if he's lucky, he has some mighty fine memories. And if he's a duck hunter, those memories are full of mallards.

As I stir up a log on my memory fire, my eyes make out in the flame the green and gray and blue and yellow of a drake mallard springing straight up from a swamp pothole to fade into the green and gray and blue and yellow of tamarack, goldenrod and sky. Or my ears pick up in the singing fire that distinctive airborne chuckle of onrushing mallards sideslipping down onto a set of decoys out of a sodden dawn.

My mallard memories begin before Opening Day with that initial annual rite of the duck hunter: fixing up the blind. No matter how sturdily you build a blind, annual maintenance is staggering. The insidious power of ice in the grip of wind and wave is something to behold. It can snap off a six-inch-thick cedar post like a matchstick. Changing marsh levels can render the floor either a foot under water or three feet above. A muskrat will likely have undermined the whole structure. Coons and birds of prey will have left their refuse. Human predators will have defaced your signs. And last year's flourishing garland of cattails and sedge will have been stripped clean by marsh gales.

After shoring up the basic edifice with due ceremony, you turn to cutting, bundling, and tying on new camouflage. We made a science of it. We cut the vegetation at a spot well removed from the blind, so as not to disturb the natural surroundings. To form sheaves, we'd construct a special sawhorse in which to cradle the bunches of grass and bulrushes while we secured them with binder twine. Each year we left this frame cached in the swamp, and each year we had to build a new one. But we really didn't mind; it was all a part of the ceremony.

So was tying the rushes to the snow-fence sides of the blind, an art known only to duck hunters. No woman arranging the centerpiece of a fancy table exercises greater care. From the perspective of every oncoming bird, the blind and its inhabitants had to be perfectly concealed. To double-check our artwork, we would row out and take a look before tying on the last batch of bundles.

With the blind rebuilt, we would engage in the most solemn preseason ritual: assuming a shooting position in the blind and praying. The power of this prayer was equal to the power of shoving ice. In no time at all, the sky would be filled with ducks, imaginary yet no less real. Far off to the left we would seem to make out the first flock as it rose off the lake and came winnowing over the railroad tracks. Invariably they were mallards. Gracefully they trailed along the far shore, swung past the south corner of the marsh, and then turned toward us as they spotted our imaginary decoys. For a moment they would hesitate, and then they were on us with a rush. We would stand, aim our imaginary shotguns, and fire, then paddle out as if to pick up the downed birds, and slowly row away. The preseason ceremony was complete. It was almost as compelling as Opening Day itself.

For duck hunters of marvelous memory, the kickoff of the hunting season was a combination of Christmas, New Year's and Yom Kippur, requiring a year of preparation. By telling tall tales around poker tables, and by repainting decoys and replacing anchor cords, duck hunters kept in mental shape even in winter. Through the summer months we reconnoitered the haunts of local mallards. Come September, you could find duck hunters painting boats that shade of ineffable beauty, dead grass tan. Dispatched to the store to buy school shoes for the kids, duck hunters spent most of the time trying on hip boots. The dedicated duck hunter also practices on his duck call. To the family and the neighbor's dog, the sounds from the basement resembled nothing ever heard on sea or land, but to the duck hunter the tones were the dulcet feeding call of the female mallard.

As opening day approached, we true duck hunters were unable to sleep, except at office desks. On The Morning, we would rise at 2 a.m. after having catnapped until midnight. Were a boss or a first sergeant to have rousted us so early, we would have resigned or gone AWOL, but since the act was voluntary, we considered it one of the four freedoms of democracy and would fix with an icy stare anybody who said we were nuts.

A memorable duck hunt is more than a simple sporting event. Rightly done, it is a ritual, as complete with sacred incantations, special garments and sacred scriptures as the most elaborate rites of a secret society. The ceremony opens at 6:15 on a late fall evening, with a TV weather reporter tracing on a map the course of a big front moving down from the Twin Cities, preceded by rain and followed by falling temperatures. At 6:20 the phone rings. It is the High Priest of the Hunt, the friend who has a private pothole.

"Did you see the forecast?" he asks. This is the countersign.

You give the password. "I sure did!"

The High Priest utters the magic words, "Let's leave at seven."

That is the signal for collecting by the numbers the biggest stockpile of combat gear this side of the Persian Gulf. Station wagon loaded, you flee the suburbs in frantic haste, like a couple of refugees deserting a doomed city. The rain beats a tattoo on the windshield, and the wind send cascades of sodden leaves across the glistening road. You don't talk much, because idle conversation might break the spell.

You turn off the highway onto a county trunk, then onto a town road, and finally onto a slippery lane. In a patch of woods you cache the car and head down through a swamp, your flashlight making only a feeble dent in the blackness as you slosh along in knee-deep muck. The rain has stopped now, but the wind keeps up its high-pitched litany in the tamaracks, punctuated once by the gabble of snow geese waving unseen overhead.

After an agonizing half-mile hike, you stumble up to a Quonset hut. The stubborn padlock finally yields to a special muttering, and you enter the mystic domain of the duck hunter: the Marsh Shack. You light the lamps, stoke the stove and set the alarm clock, all according to a routine as immutable as a baptism.

You sleep only fitfully, disturbed by the nightsounds of the swamp, and you are up making breakfast before the alarm goes off. You have to crack a film of ice on the water bucket. It will be a good day for ducks.

In the strange half-light that precedes the dawn, you load the skiffs and shove off. Largely by instinct, you paddle toward your blind. To toss out the decoys, you assume a kneeling position, an attitude of supplication vital to the ritual. As if in answer, two bluebills burst by. It is still too early to shoot. Off to the east, the dawn is wrestling with the night on a mat of low-hanging clouds. The result is a blood-red draw. A shot off in the distance marks the opening hour. You hunker down in the cattails and scan the sky.

A hen pintail is looping low, straight for the decoys. With a desperately anxious bid for companionship, she plops in, motionless for a moment, seemingly exhausted. You stand up, and she takes off, frantically wingbeating for altitude against the wind that threatens to carry her back into your blind. You fire, and she folds with that total abandon that makes the deed seem preordained. You push out for the retrieve.

It never fails! No sooner are you out of the blind than a flight of blackheads comes in right over the blocks. They must have swept down from up the river, behind you. Your first consciousness was their wing sound as they passed, low-pitched and soft, yet somehow instantly audible over the roar of wind and the splash of waves. There is no way to describe such a sound — a little like the tearing of an old brocade, yet that fails to suggest the excitement it arouses. A person hunts less for birds than for such moments.

A bunch of baldpate are fooling around over the trees on the far shore, wheeling, dropping with that old broken-wing flutter, catching themselves, flaring, soaring. These ducks give you the impression of taking to the air for the sheer joy of flight. From the right, a train of mallards interrupts your reverie. They turn in, circle your set twice, set their wings for an instant, then suddenly flare, rocketing up as if they had been shot at. You give them your most plaintive chuckle on your call. They respond nicely.

Cautiously, they look over your set again. As they pass, you give them another seductive chuckle. The leaders seem not to hear and keep climbing, but a half-dozen others veer off, make a wide swing, and then cup their wings and come weaving down as if pulled by an invisible cord. Right out in front of you they lower their big orange legs, brace their pinions and splash in.

This is the climax of the duck hunter's ceremony, always breathtaking. For one awesome second there is nothing in time but you, a little stretch of windswept pothole, and a huddle of wild waterfowl. For a magic moment, you look right into the eye of nature. The memory is forever.

The firing of your gun is strictly anticlimactic, like the benediction after a sermon. Like as not, you don't hit anything — at least that's what happened to me one particular morning. I stood up, three greenheads vaulted into the air every which way, I got off three wild shots, and not so much as a feather stayed behind. I didn't really care. The mallards had fought a good fight, and I had kept the faith. Memories are made of this.

I have another special memory of a special hunting companion.

"Daddy, will you take me duck hunting someday?"

"Why, sure, Laurie," I said.

It was easy to say yes, because it was an evening in mid-July and even though I was painting decoys in the basement, the duck season seemed a long way off. But time has a way of passing, even for an impatient duck hunter, and a ten-year-old daughter has a way of remembering just about everything. So it was that Laurie called my bluff in the middle of the next season.

Cornered like a mouse, I said, "All right, we'll go Saturday afternoon." An afternoon is no time to go duck hunting, but you can't drag a youngster down to a blind at dawn. When Laurie and I trudged down to Blank Lake, I was feeling very much a martyr to the cause of fatherhood. "Today is going to be a total bust," I thought. Little did I know what was in store. First there was the test of wits that only a ten-year-old can subject you to. Try giving intelligent answers to a barrage of questions like:

"Why doesn't a duck boat have seats, Daddy? Why is it painted all blotchy? Why don't you paddle straighter? Why are decoys called decoys? Why do you put them where there aren't any waves? Why do ducks have to land into the wind? How can you tell a duck? How can you tell a mallard from a mudhen?

"Why is the blind tilted? Why didn't you build it level? Why do you use a duck call when it doesn't sound like a duck? Where does the shot go when it doesn't hit anything? Why doesn't the lake fill up with lead? Why didn't we bring more sandwiches? How does a Thermos bottle work?"

Feeling like a guy testifying before a Congressional committee, I would never have seen those mallards if they had not ripped past with a jet-plane roar. They were riding a thirty-five-mile-an-hour wind, but they heard me call.

"Scrouch down," I told my partner. She hunched up like a veteran.

At the far end of the lake, the Canadian mallards climbed to five hundred feet, circled for one suspended moment, then headed back. Far out in front of our blocks, they started to slant down like satellites, cupped wings whistling, burnished breasts gleaming, racy heads craning.

"Take a good look, Laurie," I whispered. "Not everybody has a chance to see wild waterfowl close up on the wing."

With a final rush they were on us, and we stood up together. The drake in the lead looked as big as a Piper Cub. I got off only one shot and never came close.

"Golly, Dad" Laurie said, "that was really something."

"Yes," I winced, "but I missed."

"That's all right. He'll be something to come back to."

I remember that moment more than days full of downed drakes.

––––––––––––––––– ✻ –––––––––––––––––

Although my strenuous duck-hunting days are behind me, each Opening Day I make a sentimental journey to where it all began for me on Rock Lake at Lake Mills, sixty years ago this fall. I can't navigate a skiff anymore or survive a duck-blind seat, but I can take potluck by walking the railroad grade that separates marsh from lake.

In a way it is bad to go back. There are ghosts around an old hunting spot. Some Rock Lake ghosts died in their beds; others did not. One is MIA in a stinking Buna swamp, another in the waters off Midway, another in a Netuno cemetery. Their names are inscribed with gold stars on the plaque in the city square park, but I cannot find them where they would like to be — with me on Rock Lake marsh on Opening Day.

So, it is bad to go back. But it is good, too.

There is the same weatherworn railroad bridge that makes such a special lookout for spying on the life of the marsh. There is the blue-winged teal that cannonballs by just as did his ancestors. And there is the pair of whistling swans that customarily occupies Korth's Bay. Waterfowl don't change. With them, you can get back behind the years.

Along the grade I can even meet myself, in the form of a youngster playing hookey from school, toting a double-barrel as big as his hopes. I talk to him about the red sprays of sumac and the golden spires of tamarack. I point out how a wood duck cranes its neck when it flies, and how a hooded merganser will decoy without caution.

I talk and we wait and we watch together, and the decades wash away with the waves. There is shotgun-booming from Schultz's Bay to the north. My companion and I hunker down in the willows. Far out over the lake, we spot them — a gaggle of greenheads. Will they give us a pass or will they swing off? It is a question as old as my years yet as fresh as my compatriot's eyes. The birds keep coming. As they near the grade they start to climb, but they are in range.

"Now!" I say, and two guns speak as one. The lead drake collapses.

"Who hit him?" I am asked.

"Why, you did!" I say.

Rock Lake has spawned a new duck hunter, and I have at least one more mallard memory.

Richard Behm is a transplant from Ohio to Wisconsin. He graduated from what is now the University of St. Thomas in Minnesota and is a professor of English at the University of Wisconsin – Stevens Point. He lives in Stevens Point with his wife, Mary. The twenty acres they own in the Town of Richford, Waushara County, is their place in the north, "even though we go south to get there." Over the years, Richard's work has appeared in Sports Afield, Field & Stream, Gray's Sporting Journal, Sporting Classics, and many other magazines.

At Middle Age:
Self-Portrait in a Deer Stand

RICHARD H. BEHM

I am at that point in life where,
actuarially speaking, the days I have left
are fewer than those I have lived.
My life insurance agent no longer calls with
offers of great deals on whole life policies.
Perhaps it's because I don't have
a whole life left. But as I sit here,
I realize how important it is for me
to be connected to the land.

I have spent most of this day, my forty-sixth birthday, perched twelve feet above the ground in a tree-stand belted to an oak growing at the edge where wetland and woodland meet. Numerous deer trails criss-cross here. This morning, before she left for work, my wife, Mary, asked what I wanted for my birthday. I thought a minute. There was really nothing I needed or desperately wanted, no clothing, no big-boys' toy such as a fishing rod or shotgun or chain saw. "I'd like a buck for my birthday," I replied.

I sat in the stand for three hours this morning, watching while the sun illuminated the tops of the birch and maple. A mist rose from the marsh and seeped through the wood. It was a glorious morning, but I saw no deer. Now it is a balmy

---

October afternoon; leaves the color of butter and burnt orange flutter around me. I sit silently, watching, waiting, thinking.

I am at that point in life where, actuarially speaking, the days I have left are fewer than those I have lived. Myron, my life insurance agent, no longer calls with offers of great deals on whole life policies. Perhaps it's because I don't have a whole life left. But as I sit here, I realize how important it is for me to be connected to the land. It is, for me, a religious experience, full of the rituals of wind and moonlight: a lusty grouse drumming the sun up on a sparkling May morning; the cry of crows circling above the birch, turning from ebony to silver in the sunlight; a necklace of geese honking across the sky; a whistling swan at dusk.

It is knowing certain things, small but important, and learning more every day: distinguishing, for instance, between the rustle of the squirrel scuffling for acorns and the soft hoof-falls of an approaching deer, and telling both of these from the tick of falling leaves; knowing the bark of geese from the Jurassic gargle of the sandhill cranes from the gravelly-gobble of the wild turkey; discerning nuthatch from junco from pine siskin from chickadee-dee-dee-dee; recognizing the interrogations of the barred owl — "Who cooks for you? Who cooks for you?" — and the spectral inquisitions of the great horned owl as its deep, saturnine "Hooooo" echoes through the darkening wood.

My deer stands are placed on twenty acres of central Wisconsin woods, swamp and trout stream that we call simply The Land, and of which we have been granted temporary custody. Oh, we've paid off the land contracts, but I try not to use the word "own." I often tell people we have land, have as in to have and to hold, perhaps to be wedded to, certainly to love. The Land is in Waushara County, town of Richford, just down the road from the Hamerstrom land near Plainfield, where noted international biologists Fran and her late husband Frederick conducted much of their raptor and prairie chicken research. Fran still lives there, vibrant as ever. West of us, in Adams County, is Leopold's famed Sand County. Modest Amish farms surround us. I like the connections.

We've tried, without success, to come up with more romantic names for The Land. For a while we tried calling it The

Cabin. Problem is, there is no cabin; instead, we have a 1968 New Moon trailer, twelve feet wide by sixty long. And as for saying "We're going to The Trailer," well, you can see it lacks panache.

Perhaps it's a lack of imagination on our part, but the land will always be The Land. Once Mary and I talked of selling it, and both of us were almost in tears at the idea. It is a refuge, a place we go to mark rituals, to heal, to touch the earth and sky; it is a place of serenity and joy of the kind the Irish poet, William Butler Yeats, found at his immortal Innisfree, where " ... peace comes dropping slow/Dropping from the veils of morning to where the cricket sings."

Peace. That is what I feel, with the soft wind blowing through the pines and the coolness of evening coming on as the sun shrinks westward. I have been sitting in this stand off and on for a half-dozen days since the bow season opened. I have seen a few deer, but only one close enough for a shot. Yesterday, I moved one of the stands from the back of the land to a place in the huge pines that grow in the middle of the property. Awhile back I trimmed a path through the pines, planted many years ago in Christmas tree rows, and made a ground blind, mostly for observing wildlife. The deer, however, have taken to using the path to get from the swamp to their evening feeding area, picking up a few acorns and mushrooms as they meander through the woods.

Last night, as I watched deer approach the path through the pines, two does came within ten yards of the opening, then bolted, obviously getting a snootful of something they found alarming, if not downright offensive — namely me. A third doe, very young, approached closer before she, too, leapt back as if hit in the nose with a fistful of human stink. Instead of staying with the other does, this one broke off and wandered north, then turned around and came up to my stand from behind. She walked right up to the ladder and sniffed it, giving no sign she knew of the man in the tree drawing a bow that would be her death. As she turned broadside, I eased off on the bow.

Now, from a hard-core biological view, one might argue that killing this deer could mean eliminating an animal clearly at the low end of the gene pool. I suppose it's the twenty years I have spent as a teacher, however, that made me think perhaps this deer could learn enough in the next few weeks to ensure her survival during the upcoming gun season. If not, she'll certainly and properly end up as venison. Regardless, I did not regret letting her live. What odd predators we are sometimes, allowing, even willing, our prey to live. It is a luxury we have as ritualistic hunters, and not people who must kill or die.

That's something I have reflected on a great deal, especially in fishing. As a member of Trout Unlimited, I have always accepted the catch and release philosophy it espouses, and for the most part I still do. I confess, though, that the more I read about fly fishing, the more catch and release seems to have taken on elitist and paternalistic trappings. I picture tweedily dressed folks talking about the mystical relationship with trout, all the while failing to understand that the real mystical relationship is with the fishes' and our own mortality.

Last spring I read A. A. Luce's *Fishing and Thinking*. Luce, who was an ardent angler as well as a professor of moral philosophy at Trinity College in Dublin, argues unequivocally that the morality of fishing, including inflicting pain and taking life, is based upon the fact that we are killing for food. He writes, "The primary object of justifiable angling is to catch fish for food; there are various pleasures incidental to angling; but they cannot justify the infliction of pain or death." The logic of his arguments haunts me. If pleasure is the main object of fishing, and if we admit the obvious, that catching fish does inflict pain at some level on fish, where would we draw the line at inflicting pain on animals for our own pleasure? Would anyone countenance capturing and torturing deer because it gave someone pleasure? Luce's moral view, of course, collides with our undeniable need for resource management to sustain healthy fish and game populations. The answer lies somewhere within the heart of each of us who hunts and fishes.

These issues are not just idle speculation with me as I sit in this deer stand. I have a clear sense of my limitations. I don't hunt unless I practice — a lot. I prepare my stand and shooting lanes carefully. I know the limit beyond which I will not take a shot. And I believe in the old country maxim: if you kill it, you eat it (which explains why the squirrels are such pests at my bird feeder).

As the sun sinks lower this day and I have seen no other deer, and as the days I will be able to hunt dwindle, I wonder if I made a mistake letting that young doe wander off into the swamp. A chill is settling in as the great wheel of seasons turns toward winter. If I don't get a deer before the weather turns really damp and cold, my chances diminish, as I am certain that deer will spook when I draw the bow and they hear my aging joints creak and pop.

My thoughts turn to what it would be like if I, indeed, had to kill to ensure my family's survival. I'm sure I wouldn't be sitting here waiting for a deer to come to me. I'd be out reading the woods, stalking into the wind, seeking and taking every advantage I could. And I am certain a different set of ethics and aesthetics would apply. Squirrels? I'd eat them. Baiting? I'd do that. Taking a risky shot? Yes, if I was growing desperate. Poaching from the king's forest, trespassing, taking game out of season? Yes, yes, and yes.

Hunting and fishing are matters of life and death, and they should be. Some call them blood sport; "sport" trivializes what we do. This last spring, on opening day, I caught four brook trout from the stream that crosses the back part of The Land. They ranged from eight to twelve inches. Heeding Luce, I killed each quickly and cleanly and slipped them into my creel. I stopped at four, though the limit was five, because four were enough for Mary and me for dinner. I'd managed this feat in less than an hour by — horror of horrors — tossing fat nightcrawlers into deep holes. I could have fished more, taking the new Winston fly rod and Hardy reel out on the Mecan or the White, but I had no need to. I released most of the trout I caught during the summer. But on opening day of trout season, we ate those brookies with fresh asparagus, new potatoes, and sweet Vidalia onions. It was a celebration of life and spring.

Life and spring. Death and winter. How closely we link these seasons and their symbols. As I sit here, the coolness of evening turns slowly to the chill of night, and a faint smell of winter rises on the wind. Death. Do I fear it? Yes. No. Maybe. It was this time of year exactly twenty autumns ago that the doctors told us my mother would not live through the winter; they gave her weeks, a couple of months at best. A life-long heavy smoker of Raleighs, she collected the coupons, redeeming them for, among other things, fishing gear for my brother and me. But at fifty-two, she was ravaged by emphysema and lung cancer. She lived until just before Thanksgiving, slipping away one cold, sleet-torn night when no one was around. A proud woman, she never wanted much of a fuss made over her in life, much less in dying. I knelt by the death bed, holding her lifeless hand, praying, then kissed her cold cheek.

And I wonder about my father, who gave up smoking after my mother's death, and who turned seventy-nine last June. He's been on blood pressure medication his entire adult life, and lately he has complained of mysterious pains and tiredness, health worries that go way beyond my own growing sense of my body beginning to fail me. I think of how hard nature is in winter on the very young, the weak, the old.

Death. And then what? It's a question to ask. I am at that age where the names of former classmates have begun to show up in the obituary columns of alumni newsletters. And now I read these columns regularly. So death is certainly out there, hunting me. Always has been I guess, but I can sense him now, the way those deer nosed my smell out of the pines.

And then what happens? The images of heaven that I learned as a child will not do — people in white robes and halos, sitting on clouds, playing harps. No, they will not do. I think in heaven there must be a place to hunt on a glorious October afternoon, there must be trout streams on star-glazed nights, and stories and laughter and people we love and are loved by, and maybe a tumbler of good bourbon now and then. Heaven. By God, I think it would have to be an awful lot like this life. Which means we'd have to keep sorrow, too. Without the sorrow, without the death, life is but a shadow of a shadow, without substance or meaning.

What do I believe of the afterlife? Perhaps folk singer Iris Dement expresses it best:

Everybody is wonderin' what and where they all
   came from
Everybody is worryin' 'bout where they're
   gonna go
When the whole thing's done
But no one knows for certain
And so it's all the same to me
I think I'll just let the mystery be.

Yes, I'll just let the mystery be, though I do believe we are more than a temporary gathering of data, stardust and water. There are, however, things I know for certain. For instance, I know that aging brings special gifts, gifts I didn't expect. This afternoon, between hunting sessions, I went out jogging, three very slow miles as my second knee surgery this past January has taken its toll. I discovered, however, a freedom from the compulsion to exercise that has sometimes dominated my middle age. As I came around a corner, three deer leapt out of a patch of ragged, gold corn and bounded, tails high, across a field of mottled browns, disappearing into a ridge of dark green pines. I stopped to watch them, something I would not have done even last year because it would have slowed my time down. All a bit silly, it seems now.

I've also discovered that as I get older, time seems to accelerate. Perhaps the theory of relativity or quantum physics can explain this. But it's something I have talked about with friends my age. A week, a month, a year, they go by at warp speed. Even here, though, there is compensation in learning how to get one's priorities straight, to cherish each moment, to live in the present, to attend to things, to care more deeply about friends, relatives, strangers whose lives unexpectedly intersect ours, the rose and the sage and carrots in the garden, the woods and water, the birds, the trout and the deer.

So, as I sit in this deer stand tonight, the world seems infinitely fragile, like some huge web in which all beings and objects are palpably interconnected, where there is only this moment in all its muted glory, where the evening stars — Mercury, Jupiter, Venus, Saturn — are but dew upon a thread with my breath in pale blue balloons rising toward them.

I check my watch. It is nearly time to go. The last minutes of today's hunt and I stare hard into the marsh, expecting to see a deer in the burgeoning dark. How often it has been that in the blink of an eye a deer has appeared where I have been looking, as if magically sprung from the very ground or conjured out of thin air. But there is no apparition tonight. I will have no buck for my birthday.

I lower my bow and sit, watching the night fill up the wood. In the distance I hear the clip-clop of a horse as an Amish farmer makes his way home from the fields. At last I climb down and make my own way, joyous in the darkness, back to the trailer, crossing The Land, following the path the moonlight makes falling through the pines.

Aldo Leopold *(1887-1948) presented his visionary philosophy on conservation ethics in his* A Sand County Almanac. *A pioneer in ecology and wildlife management, he was the first to hold the chair of the department of wildlife management at the University of Wisconsin. His writings opened the eyes of the world to the sensitive and delicate balance of nature. His principles and philosophies continue to be the foundation of environmental teaching around the world. In the accompanying essay, he speaks as eloquently as anyone ever has about the value of wildlife.*

Goose Music

ALDO LEOPOLD

Babes do not tremble when they are shown
a golf ball, but I should not like to own
the boy whose hair does not lift his hat
when he sees his first deer.

Some years ago the game of golf was commonly regarded in this country as a kind of social ornament, a pretty diversion for the idle rich, but hardly worthy of the curiosity, much less the serious interest, of men of affairs. Today, scores of cities are building municipal golf courses to make golf available to the rank and file of their citizens.

The same change in point of view has occurred toward most other outdoor sports — the frivolities of fifty years ago have become the social necessities of today. But strangely enough, this change is only just beginning to permeate our attitude toward the oldest and most universal of sports, hunting and fishing.

We have realized dimly, of course, that a day afield was good for the tired businessman. We have also realized that the destruction of wildlife removed the incentive for days afield. But we have not yet learned to express the value of wildlife in terms of social welfare. Some have attempted to justify wildlife conservation in terms of meat, others in terms of personal pleasure, others in terms of cash, still others in the interest of science, agriculture, art, public health, and even military preparedness. But few have so far clearly realized and expressed the whole truth, namely, that all these things are but factors in a broad social value, and that wildlife, like golf, is a social asset.

But to those whose hearts are stirred by the sound of whistling wings and quacking mallards, wildlife is something even more than this. It is not merely an acquired taste; the instinct that finds delight in the sight and pursuit of game is bred into the very fiber of the race. Golf is sophisticated exercise, but the love of hunting is almost a physiological characteristic. A man may not care for golf and still be human, but the man who does not like to see, hunt, photograph, or otherwise outwit birds or animals is hardly normal. He is super-civilized, and I for one do not know how to deal with him. Babes do not tremble when they are shown a golf ball, but I should not like to own the boy whose hair does not lift his hat when he sees his first deer.

We are dealing, therefore, with something that lies very deep. Some can live without opportunity for the exercise and control of the hunting instinct, just as I suppose some can live without work, play, love, business or other vital adventure. But in these days we regard such deprivations as unsocial. Opportunity for exercise of all normal instincts has come to be regarded more and more as an unalienable right. The men who are destroying our wildlife are alienating one of these rights, and doing a thorough job of it. More than that, they are doing a permanent job of it. When the last corner lot is covered with tenements we can still make a playground by tearing them down, but when the last antelope goes by the board, not all the playground associations in Christendom can do aught to replace the loss.

If wild birds and animals are a social asset, how much of an asset are they? It is easy to say that some of us, afflicted with hereditary hunting fever, cannot live satisfactory lives without them. But this does not establish any comparative value, and in these days it is sometimes necessary to choose between necessities. In short, what is a wild goose worth? I have a ticket to the symphony. It was not cheap. The dollars were well spent, but I would forgo the experience for the sight of the big gander that sailed honking into my decoys at daybreak this morning. It was bitter cold and I was all thumbs, so I blithely missed him. But miss or no miss, I saw him, I heard the wind whistle through his set wings as he came honking out of the gray west, and I felt him so that even now I tingle at the recollection. I doubt not that this very gander has given ten other men a symphony ticket's worth of thrills.

My notes tell me I have seen a thousand geese this fall. Every one of these in the course of their epic journey from the Arctic to the gulf has on one occasion or another probably served man in some equivalent of paid entertainment. One flock perhaps has thrilled a score of schoolboys, and sent them scurrying home with tales of high adventure. Another, passing overhead of a dark night, has serenaded a whole city with goose music, and awakened who knows what questionings and memories and hopes. A third perhaps has given pause to some farmer at his plow, and brought new thoughts of far lands and journeyings and peoples, where before was only drudgery, barren of any thought at all. I am sure those thousand geese are paying human dividends on a dollar value.

Worth in dollars is only an exchange value, like the sale value of a painting or the copyright of a poem. What about the replacement value? Supposing there were no longer any painting, or poetry, or goose music? It is a black thought to dwell on, but it must be answered. In dire necessity somebody might write another *Iliad*, or paint an "Angelus," but fashion a goose? "I, the Lord, will answer them. The hand of the Lord hath done this, and the Holy One of Israel created it."

Is it impious to weigh goose music and art in the same scales? I think not, because the true hunter is merely a noncreative artist. Who painted the first picture on a bone in the caves of France? Who alone in our modern life so thrills to the sight of living beauty that he will endure hunger and thirst and cold to feed his eye upon it? The hunter. Who wrote the great hunter's poem about the sheer wonder of the wind, the hail, and the snow, the stars, the lightnings, and the clouds, the lion, the deer, and the wild goat, the raven, the hawk, and the eagle, and above all the eulogy of the horse? Job, one of the great dramatic artists of all time.

Poets sing and hunters scale mountains primarily for one and the same reason — the thrill to beauty. Critics write and hunters outwit their game primarily for one and the same reason — to reduce that beauty to possession. The differences are largely matters of degree, consciousness, and that sly arbiter of classification of human activities, language. If, then, we can live without goose music, we may as well do away with stars, or sunsets, or Iliads. But the point is that we would be fools to do away with any of them.

What value has wildlife from the standpoint of morals and religion? I heard of a boy once who was brought up an atheist. He changed his mind when he saw that there were a hundred-odd species of warblers, each bedecked like to the rainbow, and each performing yearly sundry thousands of miles of migration about which scientists wrote wisely but did not understand. No "fortuitous concourse of elements" working blindly through any number of millions of years could quite account for why warblers are so beautiful. No mechanistic theory, even bolstered by mutations, has ever quite answered for the colors of the cerulean warbler, or the vespers of the wood thrush, or the swan song, or — goose music. I dare say this boy's convictions would be harder to shake than those of many inductive theologians. There are yet many boys to be born who, like Isaiah, "may see, and know, and consider, and understand together, that the hand of the Lord hath done this." But where shall they see, and know, and consider? In museums?

What is the effect of hunting and fishing on character as compared with other outdoor sports? I have already pointed out that the desire lies deeper, that its source is a matter of instinct as well as of competition. A son of Robinson Crusoe, having never seen a tennis racket, might get along nicely without one, but he would be pretty sure to hunt or fish whether or not he were taught to do so.

But this does not establish any superiority as to subjective benefits. Which helps the more to build a man? The question (like the one we used to debate in school about whether boys or girls are the best scholars) might be argued till doomsday. I shall not attempt it. But there are two points about hunting that deserve special emphasis. One is that the ethics of sportsmanship is not a fixed code, but must be formulated and practiced by the individual, with no referee but the Almighty. The other is that hunting generally involves the handling of dogs and horses, and the lack of this experience is one of the most serious defects of our gasoline-driven civilization. There was much truth in the old idea that any man ignorant of dogs and horses was not a gentleman. In the West, the abuse of horses is still a universal blackball. This rule of thumb was adopted in cow country long before "character analysis" was invented and, for all we know, may yet outlive it.

But after all, it is poor business to prove that one good thing is better than another. The point is that some six or eight million Americans like to hunt and fish, that the hunting fever is endemic in the race, that the race is benefited by any incentive to get out into the open, and is being injured by the destruction of the incentive in this case. To combat this destruction is therefore a social issue.

To conclude: I have congenital hunting fever and three sons. As little tots, they spent their time playing with my decoys and scouring vacant lots with wooden guns. I hope to leave them good health, an education, and possibly even a competence. But what are they going to do with these things if there be no more deer in the hills, and no more quail in the covers? No more snipe whistling in the meadow; no more piping of widgeons and chattering of teal as darkness covers the marshes; no more whistling of swift wings when the morning star pales in the east? And when the dawn wind stirs through the ancient cottonwoods, and the gray light steals down from the hills over the old river sliding softly past its wide brown sand bars — what if there be no more goose music?

In the North, winter may arrive

any time in November, when hunting

shacks are vacant and shuttered and

no one is abroad in the land to disrupt

the feeling of solitude and isolation.

Winter

The frozen earth lies rigid,

every lake is locked in ice, and the

bare branches of aspens weave a stark

tracery against the sky.

JACK KULPA
From "Just One More"

Leroy Lintereur

(1920-95) was born in Two Rivers and grew up near the West Twin River. His boyhood was full of experiences around the river and its marshes and along the shoreline of Lake Michigan. Using a skiff called the Sea Weed, and at times setting off afoot in hip boots, he wandered the marshes, creating a relationship with what would later become a career. He graduated from the University of Wisconsin-Madison with a degree in wildlife biology; in 1954 he moved his family to northeastern Wisconsin, where he was a district wildlife game manager with the Department of Natural Resources for nearly thirty years. His popular nature column was a long-time feature in the Marinette daily newspaper.

Reprinted by permission of the family of Leroy Lintereur.

Otters

LEROY LINTEREUR

It gives me claustrophobia to think
of an otter diving this route all winter,
swept along in blackness. Do they ever
miscalculate? Is it fondness for
crayfish or love for the stream that
sends them on their way?

"I feel guilty of suckers."

So wrote Henry David Thoreau in his journal. Now, Henry hadn't really been mean to suckers. He had only failed, in his estimation, to give them proper respect and concern, an idea we can all reflect upon. I personally feel guilty of many things, suckers certainly, but particularly otters, and I never see one, or its sign, without thinking, "Here's an animal to celebrate." There is nothing ever commonplace about an otter.

We, an otter and I, had a mild happening last week. A perfect winter day is hard to define, but one where the season is not itself must come very close. Like last Wednesday. By noon, there was a slight mist in the air, just enough to blur the landscape a bit, and filter bright light pouring out of the suddenly powerful sun. The snow became tacky, caving in with each step. I shucked cap and coat, happy in the pleasant grip of a non-winter day. I expected great things, and for this, little streams are always prime.

There, the sign of something. An otter track, furrowed through snow, vivid in bright light, then vanishing into a fissure and under the ice. Then up again, through another fissure, and so on, down the stream. On a clear pan of ice it had galloped along, as if in haste to dive into the stream once more.

Occasionally you could hear a whisper of water under the snow, see it color the snow gray, and then become a black stream, open, slipping through stones and a sort of icy slush. It gives me claustrophobia to think of an otter diving this route all winter, swept along in blackness. Do they ever miscalculate? Is it fondness for crayfish or love for the stream that sends them on their way? I like to think the latter, this stream a universe, the alpha and omega of their existence.

We humans, too, respond to these streams, even in winter, when they are but a vague murmur under the snow, a rumor of water. Since the world is one, we, too, are part of their universe. But I am sure our response can never be a measure of what these streams mean to the otters. And this can apply to the world of any creature. That's why Henry felt guilty of suckers, and I, occasionally, feel guilty of otters.

Steve Hopkins *retired in 1994 after thirty-six years as a reporter, editor, feature writer, outdoor writer and columnist for* The Wisconsin State Journal *in Madison. Two collections of his writing,* The Quiet World of Steve Hopkins *and* Walter's Boy, *have been published by Waubesa Press. For more than twenty-five years, Steve and his wife, Frances, divided their time between their home in Madison and a cabin in the wooded Kickapoo Hills of Vernon County. Since his retirement he and Frances, a native of Montana, have traveled to Australia, New Zealand and Japan and have made frequent trips to Alaska and to the American West and Southwest. Travels closer to home include visits to southern and central Wisconsin trout streams that require his attention in the spring and summer. Bud Laugen, Steve's longtime friend and companion who appears in this story, died before* Wisconsin Seasons *went to press. He was 86.*

Cabin Fever

STEVE HOPKINS

There are those who seek warmer climates
in the winter. I am quite content
to stay here, in the cold and snow,
tending my woodpile and my stove,
always eagerly awaiting a good Wisconsin
blizzard to add a little spice to the days.

There is a light dusting on the cabin porch where snow has drifted in through the screen. Most of it came in last night. It rests in the corners, where the breeze has blown it, and on top of a small woodpile I leave inside to keep it dry. It rests, too, on the bare tree branches outside and on the steep hillsides that surround the cabin, covering last year's dead leaves and fallen limbs.

A set of tracks on the nearest hillside tells of my descent after a morning walk that took me around the perimeter of my thirty-nine-and-a-half acres. I'm not sure how I ended up a half-acre short of a forty. It's something that happened a long time ago, I have been told, in a trade made by neighboring farmers.

This cabin, deep in the Vernon County hills, is a place my wife and I sometimes call home. Frances and I built it more than twenty-five years ago, camping with our three young children, Peter and Katy and Jayne, in a tent pitched in a clearing while we worked. Henry Haugrud, who lives on a nearby farm and was working in the lumber yard in town at the time, more or less designed the building and would stop by evenings after work to check on our progress and sometimes to lend a helping hand.

The cabin measures sixteen by twenty-four feet, thirty-two feet if you include the porch. Henry's reasoning was simple, but it made sense. "Lumber," he explained, "comes in eight-foot lengths." It occurred to me that if Frank Lloyd Wright had applied the same reasoning, then Taliesin, the Guggenheim Museum and the Tokyo Imperial Hotel would have been rectangles. But Henry was a farmer, a countryman who lived in a world of squares and rectangles and exact measurements, of barns and granaries and pole sheds, of fields neatly enclosed by square-cornered fences. So a rectangle the cabin would be. He took the measurements and ordered the lumber. It arrived on a rainy morning early in June, delivered in a pile by the side of the road.

I had never built a cabin or much of anything before, but I had a big wooden toolbox that had belonged to my grandfather, a carpenter, and it contained everything I would need. There were saws, hammers, a square, a level, a carpenter's folding rule, calipers, a plumb bob complete with string and a chunk of blue chalk, chisels, punches, a brace and drill bits. Looking around at the dense spring woods in which we would be working, I felt that I should have carried it here by oxcart or in the bed of a covered wagon, but I unloaded it from the back of a station wagon instead, and we went to work.

It was about mid-June when we began. It was finished, at least as finished as it will ever be, on the day before the Fourth of July, in time for us to attend the parade down Main Street in nearby LaFarge and to drive up to Dean Hamilton's Rockton Bar for a barbecued chicken dinner, grilled outside near the banks of the Kickapoo River. We watched a horse-pulling contest while we ate.

Thinking of that July day now, standing on a snowy porch in my stockinged feet, reminds me that I am cold. A thermometer hanging on the porch wall reads a few notches above zero. I pick up a few pieces of wood, bang them together to knock the snow off, and go inside.

The cabin is one big room. An old Michigan stove stands on one end; two twin beds, a dresser, a shelf of books, and jackets and hats hanging on pegs occupy the other. There is a sofa, a square oak dining table covered with a red checkered oilcloth, a small work table, a refrigerator and a cookstove. We have electricity, but no plumbing. We bring water from home in five-gallon jerry cans when we come here. While we are here there is a fresh supply available from an artesian well that pours out of a hillside four or five miles away. The well is on the way to town. An alternative is the hose in Henry's milk-house.

My favorite recliner, brought from home when it was judged unsightly and replaced with one not nearly as comfortable, now sits in front of the stove, just exactly within foot-warming distance. I put a couple of chunks of oak in the stove now, adjust the chimney draft and settle into the chair. Dinner (we have breakfast, dinner and supper here) is a pot of bacon and beans simmering on the cookstove.

I have been actively enjoying this Wisconsin winter. In only the past couple of weeks I have walked for miles, along abandoned railroad beds and along city streets; and traveled on cross-country skis on maintained trails in Blue Mound State Park and in the Arboretum in Madison. I have made my own trails in the Mazomanie Wildlife Area. I have been downhill skiing and jigging through the ice for bluegills, both activities in Sauk County. In the company of Sam Robbins, a Madison birder, I spent a cold afternoon crisscrossing backroads in southern Columbia County in search of a snowy owl wintering there. A few have spotted it. We did not.

There are those who seek warmer climates in the winter. I am quite content to stay here, in the cold and snow, tending my woodpile and my stove, always eagerly awaiting a good Wisconsin blizzard to add a little spice to the days. There are a few times during the year when the cabin becomes a hunting or a fishing camp, but for the most part I come here to rest, to unwind, to walk the hills, to catch up on my reading. There is no telephone and there is no television, only a radio to keep me in touch with the world outside, should I feel the need for it.

The radio is good company sometimes during the long evenings. There is something that happens in the magic of the night atmosphere that brings in stations from around the United States and even from Canada and Mexico — music from Texas, baseball games from Chicago, Cincinnati, Atlanta and sometimes even Milwaukee. And there are crisp and bright autumn weekends, when the woods have turned to red and gold and with leaves falling gently around me, when I set the radio on the porch and listen to Wisconsin and Green Bay football games while I chop and saw away at my woodpile.

I come here for this, too, to watch the seasons unfold, to witness fall turning into winter, and then to feel the first warm breath of spring and to watch the normally dry ditch outside the cabin turn, for a time, into a flooding creek carrying the winter's snowmelt from the hillsides. It is not long then until the green shoots that have been lurking just beneath the woods floor become bloodroot and trillium and all the colorful wildflowers of spring. And then, sometime early in May, the morel mushrooms begin to sprout in hidden places in the woods, and the hunt for them begins.

If we are lucky, Frances and I, we will have at least a couple of good meals of morels, lightly floured and fried in butter. We will served them along with wild asparagus that Frances finds along the country roadsides when we travel, and maybe with some blackberry jam made the summer before from berries picked from the bushes in the woods at the edge of the hilltop meadow.

There is farming going on around us, too, in the spring, and logging, and in the late winter and early spring some of our neighbors collect the sap from the sugar maples and spend long nights boiling it over open fires until it becomes a sweet, slightly smoky, golden syrup. It is all part of rural life in this rolling Kickapoo Hill country.

I am here alone this time, but it is not always so. Frances and I are here together more often than not. Another frequent companion is Bud Laugen, an old friend some twenty years my senior who comes with me often, in season, either to fish for trout in the clear streams that run fast through the deep valleys here or to scout the hills for wild turkeys in spring and again in fall. He is good company, I suppose, because he is good at both pursuits but takes neither too seriously. In the years he has been with me we have toasted his birthdays through his late seventies and well into his eighties over brandy manhattans, which he calls "red ones," before dinner at the Viking Inn in nearby downtown Viroqua, always in the late evening and always after at least part of a day afield.

I say part of a day because we don't hunt too hard anymore. It has something to do with the hills growing noticeably steeper as we grow older. Bud claims it's because Henry and the other farmers around here spend their winters moving rocks from the valleys to the tops of the hills. So, often we begin the day early and with good intentions, if it is cold or windy or wet, and after what we consider to be a reasonable amount of time spent battling the elements, we head for the Bandbox Cafe on Main Street in LaFarge, where we might spend a good part of the rest of the morning over breakfast, reading the newspapers and catching up on local goings on with Bandbox regulars.

There have been beautiful days in early May when we have hunted turkeys in the morning and fished for trout in the afternoon in Mill Creek, just over the county line in Richland County where an early trout season was in effect.

Wild turkeys are relative newcomers to these hills, but they are a common sight here now. We see them on the hillsides and along the creeks that run through the valleys, in the mornings and in the afternoon until they head back up to their roosts. They add a new dimension to the Vernon County wildlife population, which already included ruffed grouse, woodcock, deer, foxes, squirrels, rabbits and raccoons.

It still is a thrill when I remember an early spring morning a few years ago when I sat on a ridgetop above the cabin and listened to the nearby drumming of a ruffed grouse and then suddenly heard, for the first time in my own woods, the unmistakable gobble of a tom turkey. I saw my one and only bobcat in the wild here on another morning when we surprised each other in the woods, our eyes locking briefly, freezing the moment forever in my mind, before the cat bounded away in fright, leaving me trembling in my boots.

There have been reports, too, of bear sightings in the area, most of them related to me by Henry, who I know takes great delight in pulling the ear of a tenderfoot, which I am sure is the role in which he views me. But he offered me friendship when I came here a stranger, and it is a friendship that has endured for more than a quarter-century. He and his family have looked after the cabin while we are away. He has helped me in the woods when I needed help, being more adept than I at cutting big trees and knowing almost exactly where they will fall.

And it was Henry who, on a beautiful, still and moonlit night a few years ago, arranged my first coon hunt, on which I experienced for the first time the night music, the singing of the dogs that before I had only read about. It was a sound, echoing through the hills, that seemed to belong here, in this place. It is a sound that begins the moment the dogs find the scent and increases in tempo until the raccoon either escapes or is treed. Veteran coon hunters, those who have learned the language, can follow the progress by listening to the dogs.

The hunters that night met in Henry's farmyard, dressed for the hunt in wool and flannel, in bib overalls, worn jackets and old barn boots. There were five of us, and three dogs. We headed out in two trucks, across and open field, through a creek and up into a wooded draw where the dogs were turned loose. It wasn't long until one of them found a track, and the music began. Two of the hunters, the youngest, wore miners' lamps attached to their caps and carried .22 rifles. The rest of us carried flashlights.

We followed slowly, picking our way around bushes, stumps and deadfalls. The barking increased in tempo. "They've got him now," one of the hunters said. "They're hot on the trail." The barking changed to a high-pitched "yip," and the hunters knew the coon was treed. We still were in the valley. The sound was coming from a hilltop. The hunters with rifles started up the hill on a dead run. Henry, James Daines and I, all getting a little old for that kind of activity, decided to wait it out where we were.

We sat in the dried, dead leaves and listened to the hunt above us — the excited singing of the dogs and then, finally, a shot. A half-hour or so later the hunters came back down the hill, minus the coon. "Got away somewhere," one of them said.

We hunted easier ground after that, moving to several locations in Vernon County, until near morning. We followed the dogs through cornfields and through creek bottoms thick with tag alders and willows. Altogether three coons were treed; three coons got away.

I returned to a still-warm cabin at first light of a new day. I got the fire going again, put the coffee pot on and loaded a cast-iron skillet with bacon and eggs. It had been a good night and a good hunt. Then, as now, there was a sense of belonging not just in these hills, but somehow to these hills, a feeling linked, I suppose, to my ancestral past, to a great-great-grandfather who came here before the Civil War and settled near the Richland County village of Gillingham that still bears his name, and to my own father's home farm not far away, where he grew up and where I spent many summers when I was a boy.

We brought our own family here, Frances and I, when the children were very young, in the hopes of teaching them values they might not learn growing up only in the city. They all have gone their separate ways now, and I am pleased to report that they turned out well.

These are the things I think about now, the things I remember, and maybe read in the flickering flames of a fire that warms me on this winter day, a fire that is showing signs of needing a little attention. It is snowing again when I go to the porch for more wood, the snow filling in the tracks in the lane and on the hillside. Back inside, I turn on the radio for the latest report on the weather.

With a little luck, I think, and if I don't try too hard to get out, I could be snowed in for a day or two. The possibility of cabin fever doesn't worry me. It is only something I get when I am not here.

George Vukelich *(1927-95) is best known for "North Country Notebook," his column in the Madison weekly* Isthmus *and in* Wisconsin Outdoor Journal *magazine. He published two books of the columns (still available from Madison's Prairie Oak Press), and his radio program, "Pages from a North Country Notebook," was a fixture on Wisconsin Public radio. "Notebook" often took readers to "the American Legion Bar up in Three Lakes," where Steady Eddy, the good priest, the doctor and Gene the bartender shared the news and wisdom of the day. The accompanying story is among his last writings; it first appeared after his death in* Wisconsin Outdoor Journal.

Reprinted by permission of the family of George Vukelich. The "Testament of a Fisherman" quotation appears by permission of the family of the late John D. Voelker.

Christmas at Bridge Pool

GEORGE VUKELICH

*Carl fancied that Paul and the trout were
mirror images of each other, dancing apart,
yet dancing as one. He sensed that
something indeed connected fish and
fisherman long before the singing fly line
ever joined them together.*

Carl stopped the car in the middle of the snow-
covered wooden bridge, shifted into neutral and
pulled the hand brake. In front of the car, the fresh
snow was trackless. It looked like a Christmas card.
Stopping smack in the middle of the wooden
bridge was a ritual he and Paul always performed
when they came up to fish trout here, and fishing trout here
had indeed been a large portion of their lives. This was home
water. Carl rolled down the window, and the winter air flowed
into the warm car, cold as the water below. He breathed
through his nose and stared upstream.

Paul had always said that next to being in the water, this
was the best spot from which to get what he called "a good
soaking look" at the stream. Was the water high? Was it low?
Was it muddy? Was it clear? Was there a hatch on? Were there
trout rising in Bridge Pool? From here you could almost fore-
tell what the fishing would be like that day. Carl could almost
tell. Paul always could. On this afternoon of Christmas Eve,
much of the stream was hidden by drifted snow on the shelf
ice, and a forlorn feeling stirred in Carl. Part of it, of course,
was that trout season was closed here until spring.

But part of the forlornness was that everything seemed diminished. The colors had drained from the landscape, leaving only the charcoal trunks and gray branches peeking through their snow covers. The landscape seemed lifeless, although he knew that wasn't true. There was life beneath these snows, beneath the drifts, beneath the cold waters and below the graveled bottom. But it was also true that winter was squeezing down on the north country.

The stream, too, was diminished in this season. It was far narrower than normal, squeezed thin in the sheath of its snow-covered banks. Not unlike a hardening artery, a doctor might say.

Ever since they were classmates in med school back in the sixties, Paul had preached that this was the way you had to look at something if you wanted to absorb it forever. They always took that "good soaking look" at the stream, and then took a celebratory nip from Paul's pewter trout flask, toasting the glorious hours that awaited them on the sacred water.

"A trout knows all about a good soaking look," Paul always said as they shared the flask. "Just picture a trout down there. Deep in its hidey hole. Under a ledge. Up on a feeding station. Picture yourself a trout. Watching the whole stream go by. Past your eyes. Through your gills. You have to know what is good and what is bad for you. You have to learn the difference between a piece of twig and a piece of food.

"A lot of stuff is always going down, coming down on you," Paul laughed, "whether you're a fish or a physician. You have to learn exactly what stuff has a needle-sharp hook in it."

Carl remembered how Paul looked with the mischief in his eyes. He was a seventh-grade boy trying to keep a straight face while the Seven Foot Nun was grilling him about the streamer of toilet tissue that somehow had unrolled from the back of the classroom. Underneath their surgeons' masks, they were both still seventh-grade boys, Carl knew, and naturally they had spent an inordinate part of their lives on trout streams — indeed, an inordinate time on this particular trout stream. Paul had once said that trout streams were "bright, silver strings by which our sanity hangs."

In the bright, warm seasons, they had fished this little stream every Wednesday for years. Most doctors golfed on their Wednesdays off. He and Paul fished. In the beginning, before the county put in the wooden bridge, the nearest road was a mile walk, and they had the place pretty much to themselves. Paul claimed some credit for the absence of people.

"I prescribe golf for all my patients," Paul said, "no matter what they've got. It keeps them off the trout streams."

In the beginning, before the bridge, this was an icy stream full of spring holes and lovely wild brook trout. Paul had discovered the stream by pure chance while they were poking around after grouse hunting one October day, when falling yellow leaves fluttered in the woods like butterflies. Paul had seen the trout flashing deep down in the clear pool where the bridge now stood.

"Brookies!" he yelled. "My God! Brookies!"

Following Paul's voice, Carl had fought through tangles of alder and underbrush that guarded the stream like barbed wire. He was sweaty and scratched and breathing hard when he saw Paul pointing down at the water.

"Look! Down there!" There was the pool, and there were the trout.

My God. What trout! He and Paul just sat with their shotguns and their dead birds and stared and shook their heads. The next week they were back without the shotguns, carrying their fly rods butt-first through the tangle of brush. Carl insisted Paul fish the pool first because it was Paul who found it. Carl always thought of it as Paul's Pool even after everyone else called it Bridge Pool, including Paul.

They caught big brook trout there, in the pool and in the stream. Natives. Wild as hares. "My God!" Paul shrieked. "We must have died. This must be heaven."

The spring water was so clean, so cold, they drank it right out of the stream. No one worried about *Giardia* in those days. No one knew what the hell *Giardia* was in those days. They just drank the virginal water and caught the virginal brookies.

Paul always started out by fishing Bridge Pool, lingering there, not really in a hurry to leave. "If I was fishing from up above or down below," he confided, "I couldn't wait to reach this pool. This pool is home."

The routine was to drop Paul off at Bridge Pool, and then Carl would drive the car down to the next county road, which crossed another bridge downstream. He left the car there and fished upstream to Bridge Pool, meeting Paul, who was fishing down to the car. Often, by the time they met, they had two or three nice fish apiece, and the brookies lay gilled and gutted, swaddled in cold, green watercress within the dampened Arctic creels.

It was Paul who had started putting his fish back, and naturally Carl followed. He told himself it was like a younger brother following a big brother who knew the ways of the world. He told himself it was also like Tom Sawyer following Huck Finn because you didn't want Huck to think you were a dummy. Then they stopped carrying creels altogether. Every now and again they would keep a few brookies for a meal, but not often, and only when Huck said it was all right that day to keep a few for the pan.

Over the years, the brookie population waned from over-fishing — over-keeping, Paul insisted — and then the water warmed up because the stream cover got chewed away by cows and cultivation and the runoff from the fields that were now full of pesticides and fertilizers. The brook trout vanished.

"Brookies are like canaries in the mine," Paul said. "They absolutely need cold water, clean water. They just can't live here anymore, and one day we won't be able to live here, either."

The DNR stocked the warming stream with rainbow trout and German browns and the fishing was good, albeit different. Most fishermen didn't notice the passing of the cold, clean water and the finicky brookies who had lived in it, because most fishermen had never known those old days before the stream was stocked, the days when only wild trout lived there.

Yes, Carl remembered, it had been a ritual, stopping in the middle of the wooden bridge. How many times had they done that? They would roll down the windows and Carl would look upstream and Paul would look downstream and they both sat quietly so that they could hear the water gurgling below as it sang over the upstream rocks and then whooshed into that first deep hole on Paul's side. Bridge Pool.

Then Carl would drive the car onto the crunching gravel shoulder and park it and open the trunk. He always let Paul get his gear out of the trunk first, pull on his waders, joint up his fly rod. Paul always went downstream — he called it "going with the flow" — and he always started out by fishing Bridge Pool. Carl let Paul go first because, truth to tell, he liked to watch Paul fish. Or, more accurately, he liked to watch Paul cast. Carl would close the trunk and look down on Paul casting into Bridge Pool.

Carl didn't know if those surgeon's hands had anything to do with it, but as Paul started his first backcast, in a twinkling he was transformed. His arms and legs and body flowed into curves and swirls as graceful and as beautiful as the trout gliding, pirouetting in the deep pool below. Carl fancied that Paul and the trout were mirror images of each other, dancing apart, yet dancing as one. He sensed that something indeed connected fish and fisherman long before the singing fly line ever joined them together.

Carl would stand for a few moments, hidden by the car, just watching. Invariably, Paul would land, and release, at least one trout from Bridge Pool. Then he would move into the tailwater and wave as he went around the bend and out of sight. Carl would wave, shake his head, and drive down to the second bridge to begin his own fishing.

Carl had always thought he knew Paul pretty well. But, he never knew about the headaches at all until one morning Paul was scrubbing for surgery and then had to cancel out. Another doctor who was scrubbing told Carl that Paul could have been sick. When Carl came out of OR, Paul had gone home. When Carl called, Paul was in bed. Weak, he said. Maybe flu. Something. Hospitals were always full of bugs. When Carl went to see him, Paul said it was really probably just one of his migraines. He'd had them off and on since medical school, and some of them just put him in bed. No big deal. People live with migraines. Paul said he always figured they were caused by stress.

"That's why we fish," he smiled. "Isn't it?"

Paul went back to work, and the same thing happened, only this time, he was doing a simple gall bladder, but couldn't finish and had to leave the OR. Nobody knew it then, but the very next day Paul had flown up to have one of his friends at Mayo check him over. When he came back from Rochester, Paul told Carl that they had found a tumor in his brain. It was inoperable. "Thank God it's not arthritis," Paul said. "I can fish with a tumor."

They didn't say how much time, but Paul knew. He wanted to fish more than ever. Every day. Rain or shine. Hot or cold. Carl reworked his schedule to go with him. Carl just plain took a month off, which would take them to the end of the trout season. Of course he did that because he was afraid for Paul and what could happen. He didn't want Paul driving or fishing alone. No way. When the season was over, well, Carl would do what had to be done then.

So they still came to their beloved trout stream. But Paul spent most of his time around Bridge Pool, not moving too much. Then he began to fish in his street shoes, standing on the bank, because he couldn't pull his waders on anymore. From the bridge Carl had seen Paul sitting on the bank, his legs sprawled like immobile clock hands. It was awful. Finally, Paul just lay on his back, immobile. Carl almost cried when he saw that. He didn't even think about fishing himself anymore.

One night at Paul's house, they were drinking brandy when Paul suddenly offered Carl all his fly rods, including his beloved Orvis three-weights. He also wanted to give Carl his Hardy fly reels, the whole collection, and there must have been over two dozen.

"Take them," Paul had cajoled. "It'll be an early Christmas present."

Immediately the warning bells rang in Carl's head and, without pussyfooting around, he plain out asked Paul if he wasn't thinking of suicide. For a moment it was the old Paul. "Isn't everybody?" he asked.

Before he left, Carl got Paul to promise he wouldn't do anything without talking to Carl first. Paul promised. They drank to it.

"You want the shotguns," Paul teased, "instead of the fly rods?"

Over the next three weeks, the fishing trips got to be joyless. Paul's coordination was deserting him by the day. Then came that most terrible of moments when Paul's line fell in a tangle at his shoes, and Paul flailed at the tangle with his rod. From the bridge, it looked like he was trying to kill a snake. He beat the ground, and the rod snapped. Paul was crying, sobbing. Carl ran down from the bridge. The look in Paul's eyes was awful. Patients get that look when they have seen into the abyss.

The second-to-last time they drove to the stream they never got out of the car. The last time, Paul said he really thought it was a waste of time now, and he didn't want to impose on Carl anymore. This wasn't fishing anyway. To hell with it. Paul began to sound slow, sometimes slurred. Carl called him at home every day, every night. The very night he checked, the phone rang three times, and then Paul's recorded voice came on. It wasn't the old recording. Paul had made a new one. He sounded tired, slow, but also playful.

"You have reached," Paul was saying slowly, carefully, "the former home of me. That is to say, you have reached the former home of the former me. If that's you, Carl, and who else would it be at this hour, dear friend, I left a note. It should explain everything. Then again, maybe not. Goodbye, dear doctor, dear friend. The only prescription for what ails us all is this one: So much water, so little time. Go fish."

Carl popped the trunk latch, put up the hood of his parka, slid himself out into the cold, and went back to the trunk. He took out Paul's old creel, slung it over his shoulder, closed the trunk, and walked to the railing. He stared down at Bridge Pool. The snowflakes were beginning to thicken.

In another season, Carl thought, there would be mayflies swirling just like that above the water, and fish would be slurping in the surface film below. A day like that made you feel you wanted to be here forever. Carl slipped the book out of the creel, cradling it in his parka against the flakes. Paul's collection of trout literature filled two rooms, but his very favorite writing was a single paragraph by the late John Voelker, the former Michigan Supreme Court justice who fished brook trout at his beloved Frenchman's Pond. The paragraph was titled "Testament of a Fisherman."

When Paul had found it, he had screamed, "Eureka!" and read it to Carl on the way to the stream. Paul had Voelker's

Testament framed and hung it on his office wall, surrounded, as Paul put it, "by my other diplomas." His patients saw it every day. The golfers couldn't understand it. Carl began to read as Paul had requested. It was aloud, but just above a whisper because that's all he could manage. A whisper was all right because Carl felt Paul was standing there anyway.

"I fish," Carl began, "because I love the environs where trout are found, which are invariably beautiful, and hate the environs where crowds of people are found, which are invariably ugly; because of all the television commercials, cocktail parties and assorted social posturing I thus escape; because, in a world where most men seem to spend their lives doing things they hate, my fishing is at once an endless source of delight and an act of small rebellion; because trout do not lie or cheat and cannot be bought or bribed or impressed by power, but respond only to quietude and humility and endless patience; because I suspect that men are going along this way for the last time, and I for one don't want to waste the trip; because mercifully there are no telephones on trout waters; because only in the woods can I find solitude without loneliness; because bourbon out of an old tin cup always tastes better out there; because maybe one day I will catch a mermaid; and finally, not because I regard fishing as being so terribly important, but because I suspect that so many of the other concerns of men are equally unimportant — and not nearly so much fun."

Carl closed the book, slipped it back into the creel, and took out the new container. He opened it, stared into it. He took off a driving glove and scooped his bare hand into the ashes. They felt grainy, dusty, coarse, like Oxydol. Carl wanted to say something memorable, something special, but couldn't. Paul would understand.

"You always said," Carl said, "the old judge was a hard act to follow. Amen."

Carl opened his hand and Paul's ashes spilled down to the stream. Carl's eyes blurred, and the ashes merged, transformed into a shimmer that looked like summer mayflies.

"Go with the flow, doctor," Carl said. "Go. Get a good soaking look."

He turned the container upsidedown, shook it gently, and Paul's earthly residue came pouring out, scattering like smoke, unfurling like some graying, weathered prayer flag in the white flakes.

Carl squinted to see through his tears, and he knew he was on the verge of losing it. It was then that he felt Paul's strong hand on his shoulder, and it was then that he heard Paul's strong voice in his ear. *There, there, doctor. There. There. Come back with the Orvis three-weight.*

The ashes floated only seconds and then sank below the surface. Carl saw that the specks and particles of ash were tiny planets, tiny moons, a newborn galaxy. It was elongating, expanding, merging into that timeless universe where hatching insects and watchful trout and eternal, moving waters dance and tumble and are accepting of everything that comes and of everything that goes with the flow. Then the ashes were gone, downstream, and around the bend.

In the car, Carl shivered, warmed his bare hand in the hot blast from the heater, and looked downstream one last time. The snow was falling more thickly, and that helped. It still looked lonely, desolate, but it also looked the way it should look up in the north country in December.

He rolled down the middle of the narrow road carefully. Between commercials for last-minute shoppers, most of the stations were playing Christmas music. One was playing polkas. Somehow, that was making him feel much better. He listened to the polkas until the young woman read the sign-off and then wished everyone a Merry Christmas, "wherever you are." Amen to that, Carl said out loud.

By the time he reached the highway, it was dark, and Carl flashed onto the times they had driven home in the dark from trout fishing in the warm nights of June. Of July. Of August. Now he could see lighted Christmas trees in the houses along the road, and he knew folks were guarding this night's warmth like gold.

He put in a tape and listened to Pete and Arlo singing. They sang "Precious Friend," all the way home. Carl sang, too.

Dan Small *A photograph convinced Dan to move from his native upstate New York in 1972 to take a teaching job at Northland College in Ashland, on the shores of Lake Superior. That photo, on the inside cover of the 1971-72 college catalog, showed a graduate in his cap and gown holding the world-record brown trout, caught on Commencement morning. Dan has been pursuing a record trout of his own in Wisconsin waters ever since. He taught French, Native American literature and various writing courses at Northland from 1972 to 1995, and was Outdoor Writer in Residence from 1988 to 1995. His son, Jonathan, is a student at Northland. Dan is host and producer of the popular "Outdoor Wisconsin"* TV program and edits the biweekly Wisconsin Outdoor News. *A widely published freelance writer, he now lives in rural Ozaukee County with his wife, Shivani Arjuna, a Vedic astrologer and holistic health practitioner, and their five cats.*

The Day the Ice Went Out

DAN SMALL

A soaking in Lake Superior's frigid waters
would mean certain death if we
happened to get stranded on a floe.
I grabbed our gear and commanded
Jonathan to start pulling his sled
straight for shore as fast as he could.

WASHBURN — A score of fishermen were rescued from the ice off what is called the S-curve railroad underpass between Barksdale and Washburn early Sunday afternoon when the ice split and left the fishermen marooned on ice separated from the shore by about fifty feet of water.

Ashland Daily Press

I really should have known better, but my six-year-old son and I were eager to get in on the hot trout action. The season's first ice was forming on Lake Superior's Chequamegon Bay, and local fishermen were taking some nice splake and browns.

The day before, we had trudged half a mile to a tiny inland lake in search of bluegills, but the fish had not cooperated. The four inches of ice on that little lake supported us easily, but Jonathan and I drilled hole after hole and jigged teardrops all morning to no avail. The next morning we decided to try the new ice on Chequamegon Bay near our Washburn home.

We arrived at the old S-curve between Washburn and Barksdale about 8:30 a.m., and I had trouble finding a place to park.

"We should have started earlier," I thought, as I surveyed the scene. Out on the ice, a small village of teepees already housed a couple dozen fishermen. Others sat on sleds, upturned buckets and folding stools, tending tip-ups and jig rods. I guessed the ice was safe, and the word was out.

A cold snap several days before had spread a skin of ice halfway across the bay. Until today, only a few brave souls had ventured out, but they had caught fish and, more important, had made it back safely. Nobody really wants to be the first to test new ice, but not many fishermen want to miss out on the fast action that first ice offers. Old hands say it is the best fishing of the season. So, after two days of watching the foolhardy reap the easy pickings, seasoned ice anglers had turned out in force, and we were among them.

Jon and I were so eager to start that I paid no attention to the southwest wind, which had been growing steadily stronger since seven o'clock and now was whipping along at a good twenty miles per hour. I was glad I had thought to borrow a teepee, and I reasoned that we would be snug inside like the rest of the guys who were already out there, no doubt hauling in trout hand over glove. With our bait and gear towed on Jon's sled and our borrowed shelter on my shoulder, we headed for the teepee village.

We crossed two or three pressure cracks, but those are always present when the ice is new, so I wasn't worried.

Perhaps I should have taken it as an omen when the top to our foam minnow bucket flew off and began rolling downwind across the bay. I dropped the teepee and took off after the bucket lid, thinking it would fall over and I could retrieve it. But the lid gathered speed and, true as a wheel, raced out of reach and then out of sight.

Half a mile out, we began passing fishermen, and I saw that the village was really a sparse settlement sprawling over some forty acres. I also saw that some of them were catching fish, and I could almost feel the tug of that first good fish of the season.

"I think we're going to see some action, kiddo," I told my son. A wide grin was his only reply. We would see plenty of action, all right, but not the kind I had in mind. I had enough wisdom to stop somewhere near the center of the teepee town, a hundred yards or so beyond most of the fishermen, but a good quarter mile closer to shore than the pioneers who had staked their claim over deeper water and, I thought, on more treacherous ice.

"Let's fish right here," I announced, and set down the heavy teepee. Grabbing my ice auger, I was startled to punch through to water with only two turns of the handle. I knelt to examine the hole and discovered the ice was only two or three inches thick. That isn't a heck of a lot for fishing on Lake Superior, but after all, it was supporting thirty or forty other guys. I decided it was safe and set to work putting up the teepee. I knew how to set it up, but had never before done it in a stiff wind. As I struggled with the canvas, I felt as if I were wrestling with a giant bat.

"If I ever get this thing together, it'll probably fly me across the bay," I thought as I stood inside the teepee and tried to fasten the cross braces, while the wind beat the canvas around my legs. Preoccupied with the teepee, I didn't hear the ice boom (Jonathan told me later he thought someone was shooting off firecrackers) and could not make out the first frantic shouts of fishermen in closer to shore. But something caught my eye, and I looked up to see one man waving his arms over his head. A shock ran through me when I understood his shouts.

"The ice is moving out!" he yelled.

The offshore wind had broken off a large sheet of ice, and we were on it! If any wave action got started, the thin ice would break into pieces like so much peanut brittle.

My first thought was to get my son to shore. A soaking in Lake Superior's frigid waters would mean certain death if we happened to get stranded on a floe. I grabbed our gear and commanded Jonathan to start pulling his sled "straight for shore as fast as you can."

As we passed other fishermen still in their teepees, I shouted, "Get to shore, the ice is moving out!" Dozens of fishermen tore down teepees, jerked out tip-ups, and threw their tangled gear onto sleds as they rushed to save their equipment and their lives. For the first time, I was glad we had been late getting started that morning. Because we had not yet begun to fish, we were among the first to start running for shore. And we had a long way to go. Jonathan could not move very fast dragging the sled, so I grabbed the rope and told him to run but to stay close to me. We were moving faster, but running straight into the wind. My lungs burned with each panting gulp of cold air. There were more thin cracks now than when we had come out, so we crossed them more carefully than before. We came to one crack a foot wide and stopped momentarily. I urged Jon to jump across with me. The ice held.

Now I became vaguely aware of others running alongside and behind us, but my attention was riveted on a group that had stopped a hundred yards ahead. As we neared them, I saw why. They had come to the spot where our ice sheet had freed itself from the ice still attached to shore. The split of water stretched in either direction as far as we could see and cut us off from shore a quarter-mile out. Then one fisherman to my left made the crossing. I ran to the spot, but the crack there looked as wide as it was near us, where five feet of open water stared us in the face.

As I turned back, three fishermen towing a heavy sled passed us and ran along the crack to our right. Then I noticed that the ice sheet we were standing on was moving parallel to the stationary shore ice, and I felt a glimmer of hope.

"Look," I said to a man who had just come puffing up to us. "The ice we're on is moving. Is it likely to jam up against the shore ice so we can cross?"

"I don't know," he replied glumly. "I've never done much ice fishing, and if I get off this lake it'll be along time before I try it again."

"Great!" I thought. "Here we are, a bunch of rookies out on a day when the experts stayed home."

But then I noticed the three guys with the heavy sled waving and pointing to the crack. Sure enough, the floe we were standing on was moving up against the shore ice. As we watched the two sheets grind together, chunks of ice six feet long broke off and piled over the crack where open water had threatened only a moment before. One of the trio tested the jam with a spud bar, then the three pushed the sled across.

"Go! Go!" I yelled to Jonathan. "Run across on those chunks!" I wanted him safely across before I tried to make it with the teepee and sled.

One of the three men who had just crossed turned back to give the boy a hand, but he scooted across the jam on his own. Then I took a deep breath and scrambled across ice chunks that jutted out where the crack had been. The sled miraculously followed without tipping over. I let out a whoop, then turned and saw the admitted neophyte still standing on the other side of the jam. "Come on!" I yelled to him. "Cross right where we did." He finally did, and the six of us headed for shore. Winded, but elated at our narrow escape, we moved more slowly now and tested the narrow cracks we came to before crossing them.

Others were not so fortunate. Before anyone else could cross, the big crack reopened, this time for good. We finally made it to shore where a mixed mood reigned among the lucky half who, like us, had got off the ice. Happy to be ashore, most expressed concern for the twenty or so still stranded. The ice had stopped moving, but yards of open water now separated the floe from the shore ice at the crack's narrowest point.

Rescue operations began almost immediately. Several lakeshore residents had witnessed the plight of those stranded and brought out rowboats. In less than two hours, the stranded fishermen and their gear were all ferried safely across the open water. Sleds, a snowmobile, and even an ATV also crossed in the boats without incident. One fisherman fell in trying to jump the crack, but his companions plucked him out and got him to shore, where his truck heater warmed and dried him as he watched the rescue along with the rest of us.

"That's quite a boy you've got there," said a man who had seen us cross the jam.

"He's pretty tough," I said. "But he was scared for a while there."

"I was pretty scared myself," the man admitted. Most of those I talked to were sobered by the incident and planned to sit out the next few days, at least, and wait for better ice conditions. I tried to give away a bucket of live shiners, but got no takers. Even a scare like that would not keep the diehards away for very long, though. One young angler just shook his head in disgust and muttered, "Man, they were just starting to bite."

As for me, I learned my lesson about thin ice. I did my share of ice fishing later that winter and caught a few decent fish, but not until the ice on the bay was a good six inches thick. And I stayed home on windy days. Of course, I told my wife what had happened — more or less — but she didn't get all the details until after the ice-fishing season.

Galen Winter, *an attorney, began his legal career representing United States businesses while living in Latin America. In 1972 he left a corporation counsel position in Chicago and hung up his shingle in Shawano, a small central Wisconsin city "where a man can associate with dogs and shotguns without arousing too much suspicion." Galen's brand of humor has been a fixture in outdoor magazines for years. His column, "The Major," appears in* Shooting Sportsman, *and another column, "Backlash," was a long-time feature in* Wisconsin Sportsman *and* Wisconsin Outdoor Journal.

The Winter of Our Discontent

GALEN WINTER

Frankly, it's hard to build real enthusiasm for any program that consists of freezing one's butt while trying to eat a frozen sardine sandwich and quench one's thirst with an icy can of congealed beer.

No doubt about it, friends. The late winter is a very tough couple of months. The snow gets higher and higher. The driveway gets narrower and narrower. The woodpile gets farther and farther away from the back door. Men find themselves home every weekend, staring out the window, drumming their fingers, looking for something to do and, ultimately, trying to be helpful to the spouse.

Women seem to become more irrational during this time of year. The more men try to help out around the house, the more hysterical the women become. By March they are regularly found seated alone in the kitchen trying to recall the lyrics of "I'll Be Glad When You're Dead, You Rascal, You." The divorce rate climbs.

For most of us, January and February are, indeed, weary, stale, flat and unprofitable. The days creep by and it seems as if spring will never come. Men go mad floating in this doldrum, this Sargasso Sea located between the closing of deer and the opening of trout season.

They do weird things, like making Prohibition the law of the land (January 20, 1920), or destroying civilized men and women's supply of good Havana cigars by allowing Castro to take over Cuba (January 1959). And, you will recall, most of our elected officials take office in January. The explanation for all this silliness is: It's cabin fever time.

Our ancestors tried to come to grips with the disease, but the best they could do was produce a rather questionable home remedy. It consisted of heavy dosages of sulfur with molasses, usually administered in March when the disorder was at its height. It was such an unpalatable and disgusting concoction that, once choked down, it took the patient's mind off the sickness for at least two weeks. By that time there had usually been enough warm temperatures to allow the patient some out-of-doors activity, and the virus had died of natural causes.

I suspect the Colonial custom of bundling* was developed as a direct result of cabin fever. It was cold outside, and there wasn't much else to do.

Though the malady has been with us for centuries, science has been able to produce neither antidote nor curing serum. In this enlightened age of governmental research grants and Medicare, those who suffer from cabin fever have been abandoned. No telethons for us. We are left to our own devices.

Some people cut holes in the ice during the first quarter of the year. Then they try to fish through them! Many other people are convinced those who participate in such enterprise should have their names placed on the waiting list of applicants for permanent residency at the funny farm.

However, contrary to such widespread belief, ice fishermen are not necessarily feeble-minded folk — you know, the kind who go snipe hunting with a bag and a club and vote for liberals. Modern experts in the field of abnormal psychology (the type of people who study peculiar phenomena, like ice fishing) contend ice fishermen are normal. They argue ice fishing is only a tactic adopted by out-of-doors types as a diversion calculated to take their minds off the debilitating effects of cabin fever.

Well, you can't prove it by me. I tried ice fishing once in February in the hope it would diminish the intensity of the attack of the particularly virulent strain of the bug that annually assaults me. Let me tell you, comrades, it was not a pleasant

---

*Bundling was a Colonial custom involving unmarried persons of opposing sexes sharing the same bed while fully clothed. The practice accounts for the rapid growth of Colonial populations.

---

experience. To begin with, I did an awful lot of chopping before I had a hole with a large enough open area to allow a reasonable cast of my fly. And there was no hatch to speak of. I didn't catch anything. I didn't even have a short hit.

Frankly, it's hard to build real enthusiasm for any program that consists of freezing one's butt while trying to eat a frozen sardine sandwich and quench one's thirst with an icy can of congealed beer. Fishing through the ice may take your mind off the boredom of the season, but so does butting your head against a stone wall.

Outdoor types who behave in an unremarkable manner nine months out of the year are capable of performing strange and aberrant acts during the cabin fever season. For example, rational people, of course, consider dancing to be an activity only slightly less repulsive than stealing pennies from the eyes of the dead (but it is preferable to public association with Congresspersons).

This attitude is based on the fact that most sane people have a hard enough time of it trying to stand upright without engaging in the two-step, the three-step, or whatever other convoluted foot movements become necessary to commit the still legalized pursuit termed dancing.

Now then, consider the garden variety sportsman who each year, on average, falls in a trout stream six times, trips four times while chasing upland game, and stumbles to the ground three times on each drive during the deer hunt. He will seldom, if ever, engage in dancing and must, therefore, be considered a rational human being.

Now imagine this same rational person suddenly throwing all caution to the wind, strapping seven-foot-long boards to his (at best) shaky feet, and charging off across the snow fields and into the winter woods. One couldn't be more surprised if he stood in the middle of a January street, dropped his trousers, and burst out singing "La Dona E Mobile."

No, friends, cross-country skiing is not rational behavior. It is performed only by those who have temporarily taken leave of their senses — that is, victims of cabin fever.

The first one-quarter of the year is, truly, a terrible time for those who like to poke around in the great out-of-doors. We are forced to fish through the ice or cross-country ski. (I've tried to revive bundling, but have met only limited success.)

In Richard III, produced around 1600 (and probably in January), William Shakespeare wrote, "How weary, stale, flat and unprofitable seem to me all the uses of the world. Fie on it. Oh, fie. 'Tis an unweeded garden that grows to seed. Things rank and gross in nature possess it merely."

Don't tell me Shakespeare didn't understand about cabin fever.

Dion Henderson *(1922-84) was a student of Aldo Leopold, a close friend of Mel Ellis, and himself a major Wisconsin literary figure. His forty-eight-year writing career revolved around his work for the Associated Press, which he joined in 1942. A native of Lake Mills, he became chief of the AP's Milwaukee Bureau in 1967 and remained in that position until his death. He sold his first short story to a national magazine at age fourteen and in his lifetime published hundreds of stories and essays in such magazines as* Field & Stream, Argosy, The Saturday Evening Post, Playboy, *and* Defenders of Wildlife. *He also wrote eight books and helped develop many young writers while editor-in-residence at the Marquette University College of Journalism. Dog stories, like the accompanying selection, were among his specialties.*

Brute's Christmas

DION HENDERSON

*Kids and dogs have one thing
in common: They do not go bad
without a reason. I have a theory
that there is a solution to every
such problem if you can find it,
and it would be nice to add
that there are no exceptions.
But there are exceptions.*

When I set down Suzie's pan of meat and meal she waggled politely, and when I put down the puppies' dish they all fell promptly and thankfully into it with all four feet. But when I shoved Brute's dish inside his pen, he looked at me sullenly a moment, then went over and lay down in the corner. He would have gone outside, but the runway drops were down for the night against the winter wind. I shut the gate and left him, knowing that after I had left the kennel he would eat what he wanted and spoil the rest out of pure cussedness.

A man knows naught of what a dog may love, nor why. A dog may forgive you bad temper and a heavy hand and thoughtlessness, and never reproach you for underfeeding or overwork, because he is a good dog and has made a decision for himself and will abide by it. On the other hand, a dog may hold your best in cold contempt and stalk past your luxuries, holding against you some mortal offense of birth — his, yours or both. There is no telling about such a dog, except that he does not want to be a good dog.

So it was with Brute. He wanted to be a mean, bad-hearted, no-good dog, and he was notably successful. You could force him into a kind of slovenly compliance with commands, but it wasn't worth the effort. And if you attempted to cross the border into intimacy, he bristled into active hostility. Only when he was left alone did he seem satisfied. He was no trouble then, but quiet in the kennel, content to eat and sleep and mind his own business. When I put the snap on the kennel door and walked up the drive toward the house through the crisp winter darkness, I wondered for the hundredth time in six months why I continued to keep him. Then I wondered why in tarnation I ever interrupted the perfectly competent trainer who had been going to shoot him as hopeless, and after that I speculated despondently on why it should take so long for such manifestations of insanity to rise through the murky depths of a Caledonian soul like mine.

There was no moon that night, but there was enough snow in the woods to make walking easy. I looked at the stars, very intense in the moonless sky, and hoped idly that we would have a white Christmas, for the kids' sake. Then I thought about Brute again, how sullen he was, a miserably unhappy dog.

Kids and dogs have one thing in common: They do not go bad without a reason. I have a theory that there is a solution to every such problem if you can find it, and it would be nice to add that there are no exceptions. But there are exceptions.

Among people who handle dogs there is a word: unbiddable. It is a term of convenience, used as though it applied to dogs, when it really covers a whole situation with a dog and a man in the middle. Now, people who handle dogs are as imperfect as anyone, and more so than most; and although dogs as a whole are very understanding and patient and forgiving about the mistakes you commit upon them, sometimes a dog is not. But because you make so many mistakes, when you have a resentful dog it is hard to remember all the mistakes accurately and be able to sort them out so that you can label the ones that made him resentful. It is a great deal of trouble, and sometimes it is quite impossible. If you cannot eradicate the resentment the dog feels over the mistake you can't remember, you have a dog to whom you apply the word "unbiddable," as though something were his fault instead of yours.

Now, the best thing to do when you have an unbiddable dog is to get another dog and hope that neither of you makes the same mistake again or that this dog is more broad-minded about human frailties. You generally take the unbiddable dog and present him to someone you don't like very well, where he either will turn out very badly and you can point to him as though the other fellow spoiled him, or he will turn out very well and the other fellow will be so much in your debt that you can afford to be rude to him openly. Sometimes, though, you find a dog who is offended by everyone he meets, and he will not forgive anybody anything; but you keep trying, and in the end you have a bad dog.

After six months it looked as though there was no goodness in Brute, or at least no key to it. Then I tried to make something good out of his badness. At least, I said, the kennel was safe with him inside. He was big for a setter, jugheaded and not afraid of anything. I had reached the point where I would settle for his being a kennel guard, which isn't much, but I am a very hard loser when it comes to dogs.

One night I came home late from town, and Betsy asked, "Who did you send down to the kennel this afternoon?"

"No one," I answered.

She shrugged. "I thought I saw someone down there. Maybe the paper boy stopped to look at the pups. Perhaps it was just shadows on the snow."

Our kennel is back on the edge of the big trees, and it's easy to make a mistake like that. But I guess it wasn't a mistake, because a day or two later the kennel door was hanging open when I came home. It had been fastened loosely with a padlock on an old stapled hasp, which had been pried loose. I scratched my head, looked inside to count the puppies, was greeted with a morose grumble from Brute, and withdrew, reassured that whoever had been snooping was likely scared half to death.

The reassurance didn't last long. We sat around after dinner thinking of all the other times someone might have gotten into the kennel, if Brute was really failing to sound the alarm.

Anyway, the more we thought about it the more we worried about the pups, and I wound up rigging an alarm that didn't have any emotional problems — a trip wire at the kennel door connecting with a buzzer in the house.

It went off in the middle of a blizzard a couple of nights before Christmas, so there was some delay in our response. I pulled on an overcoat and boots and fought through the drifts to the kennel. There was a considerable uproar, the pups yelling in various tones of soprano, and Sue glowering in her corner. I turned on the lights and counted the puppies thankfully. They were all there. Then I saw the open door. Brute was gone!

I turned out the lights and went back to the house. When Betsy heard about it, she said, "You ought to hurry and get a new lock on the door."

"Before they come back for the pups?"

"No, before they return Brute."

For a moment I felt the same way. But I do not like dog thieves, even the unlucky ones. A man who steals a dog does not just take a more or less valuable piece of property away from you. The objection is not so substantial as that. It has something to do with the feeling that a sporting dog is the product of many generations of both dogs and men, that he is something that resulted from a combined effort down the years to refine and perfect a quality as intangible as emotion and as enduring as fame.

When a dog is stolen out of his registry, something is taken away from the dignity of those past men and dogs who cannot defend themselves. Of course, most dogs are end products in themselves, because the quality they have is not more than they need, and they do not have any to spare when the time comes to pass it on. But as long as you have a dog, you keep thinking that perhaps some miracle of experience will open the door of ancestral reserves and allow him to be everything his bone and blood promised for him. Thus a man who steals a dog is a man who monkeys with dreams he knows nothing about, and generally is a reptile at heart.

When I finished thinking about this, I was good and mad. Not many tracks were left by morning; drifting snow had done a good job on the trail. The thief had apparently kept to the driveway when he left. Where the drive paralleled the Norway windbreak you could make out some sign. There were some dog tracks, and I thought the explanation for Brute's meekness might be explained by these, if they belonged to some lady dog who had been used for bait. But the tracks looked mighty like Brute's own. Only of course no one could control Brute without a leash, off the field, and this dog had been loose, by the wide pattern of the tracks. Anyway, it was a clean getaway.

I went back to the house and changed my clothes to go into town and have a few choice words with the sheriff. Tracing a dog like Brute would be quite a problem, because no one knew him or cared about him. A famous dog is relatively safe, at least from professional thieves, because trying to hide a dog whom a million or so people can identify on sight leads to a very confined old age. Only very stupid people steal very famous dogs, and when it happens, as it did to Sue's great daddy, it is because the predatory nitwit who took him didn't know one dog from another.

Just as I was getting ready to leave the dog house, someone knocked on the back door. It was a tall, lean man in an old Army overcoat and a broad-brimmed hat with a big scarf wrapped around it from the crown down under his chin, on account of the wind. He had a kid with him, and the kid wore a coat made of an old Army blouse and a big scarf, too, but no hat. The man looked vaguely familiar. Then I recognized him. He was the back-country stranger who had built himself a cabin in the tamaracks the summer before and started a grimly independent existence raising hogs and chickens.

"Come on in," I said. "Betsy, break out some Christmas cookies."

"Nope, thank you," the man refused. "Ain't going to set. Jed here has just got something to say."

"Yessir," little Jed said. His nostrils were pinched, and what I could see of his face would have been pretty white even without the cutting winds. "I stole your dog, sir," he addressed the doorknob with a stony stare. "I came onto your place unbidden, and I stole your dog, and I'm purely sorry."

He was certainly having a terrible time, and with good reason. So long as it had been a kid's doing, and had turned out this way, I stopped being mad.

"There were some mighty fine pups in that kennel," I said as gently as possible. "You didn't bother them."

"There's some folks," little Jed flashed back, "as don't know a good dog when they see him."

"Jed!" the man spoke sharply. "Mind your manners, boy."

"Yessir," the kid addressed the doorknob again.

I coughed a little from the wind and asked, "Where is the dog?"

"Here," the boy replied. He put his fingers in his mouth and whistled sharply, and I'll be darned if Brute didn't come bouncing up the driveway merrily as a pup, stop companionably by the kid, and wag his tail. The kid's hand — clean, I noticed, but blue with cold — reached out and patted the ugly head. And Brute, so help me, licked the hand. At that, little Jed suddenly broke down, knelt in the snow, weeping, planted a wild kiss on Brute's unbeautiful nose, then fled down the driveway.

The dog started to follow, and the kid turned, shouting, "Go back, darn you!" Brute obeyed.

I leaned against the door, not feeling the wind any more, and tried to compose myself to some sort of resignation to loss of reason. This couldn't be happening! I believe in miracles, but in the modest six-bit variety rather than the large economy-sized, super-deluxe model like this. After seeing Brute wag his tail and lick someone's hand, I would have stood unstartled while little people sailed through the air on gossamer wings, picking purple flowers on the snow.

Jed's father was still standing there, a stern-looking man who had not spent much time laughing, maybe never had it to spend. He looked as though he was dreadfully embarrassed by what his boy had done, but was a little proud of how he'd done at the end, and I didn't blame him a bit.

He said formally, "You reckon you got satisfaction?"

"About the way the dog left and how he came back," I said just as formally, because there is a way to talk to these proud men. "After a while, I'll stop at your place, and maybe we can talk a little."

"If'n you'd care to." His face had changed a little. "Right now me and mine still stands in the light of trespassers." Just in time, I understood he was making a Biblical reference.

I let a day go by before I followed it up. Betsy grumbled at the delay, because Christmas was coming. She had overheard the session when little Jed and his dad brought Brute home, and I had to take an oath I'd try to do something about it before she'd let me into the house. Around our place, we don't ordinarily sell mature dogs, but I had a notion I wouldn't have much luck trying to give one away in this case. I was right. Jed's dad was very polite, very formal and inflexible. When I stepped into the desolate little cabin, Jed gave me that impersonal stare of a hurt youngster and nodded stiffly. Jed's mother didn't say much; neither, as a matter of fact, did Jed's dad.

"Ask the boy."

Jed said firmly, "No, thank you kindly, sir, we 'uns don't take no charity nor no presents like that." A couple of tears squeezed out, and he got up and walked outdoors.

His dad said in farewell, "I'm obliged to you for the offer, and I'll thank you not to mention it again. This here's a hard world, and I can't no wise keep my boy from finding it out sooner or later."

I allowed that was true enough, and we parted with all the ceremony of a couple of old-time diplomats.

At home again, I stopped at the kennel and looked at Brute. He was sulking in his pen, morose as usual, but with something more, too. He was hurt and unhappy. You get so that you can tell, and in a way it's a good sign. A dog who does not love anything is like a man in the same condition: he cannot be hurt at all, and that makes him either a very good workman or a very bad one, and one is nearly as unsatisfactory as the other unless you are looking for a special kind of workman. But once a dog or kid or man feels bad about the way something has turned out, you know that he has been touched in his heart, and if ever you want him to take up his responsibilities, you will lose the only chance you have a right to expect.

So I stood looking at the ugly Brute, not knowing what communication there was between him and little Jed, and — worse than that — not knowing how to keep them from losing it and leaving the kid bitter and resentful, too. Presently I was pretty mad again, but this time at the world in general, because it makes tough rules that kids have to grow up and learn. That's about as futile a way to waste time as there is; so I gave Brute an extra ration of meat that I knew he wouldn't eat anyway, and stamped up to the house.

Betsy was stringing Christmas decorations, and the kids were in a panic because the fireplace was very sooty and Santa Claus was bound to get his suit all dirty. My child Amy said that not only was she worried, but so was Sam, who is maybe the world's most famous shorthair when he isn't snoozing on Amy's bed. As a matter of fact, Sam did look worried when Amy mentioned it, and I sought refuge by helping Betsy before Amy went into it any further. For some reason, I never have just a nice, comfortable, average dog. Either they're Brutes or they're Sams, who can make me feel quite backward and uncouth whenever they want to.

We had a lot of fun decorating the house and teasing the kids. Then I remembered Jed and the cabin in the tamaracks, and it wasn't so much fun anymore. I told Betsy what I'd found out: how Jed had been coming in through the woods to the kennels all fall and winter, talking to Brute through the wire, sometimes for hours on end, and how he'd finally broken in once and taken the dog out, but brought him back, conscience-stricken, before he got all the way home. And then how he'd finally come back and taken him for good, and how he ran away from his dad when he found out, and his dad had tracked him relentlessly through the storm that morning before they brought Brute home.

After that, we did not talk about it anymore, because I have known lonely men like Jed's pa before, and you do not push them into doing things.

Then it was Christmas Eve, with the kids in bed and the house full of people making the annual holiday rounds, standing around the bowl on the buffet and singing. Suddenly there was a knock on the back door. Jed's dad stood there, his face bleak in the reflected light. It was snowing a little, and the crystals melted on his jaw.

"Admire to have a word with you," he said. "I hate to mention business on a night like this."

"It's all right," I said. "What kind of business?" It was an effort for him to get it out. "Sort of wondered whether you'd sell me that dog."

I didn't answer so fast. This was a time to tread lightly and let policy look after itself.

"I might," I said. "For a fair price. He's a high-bred dog."

He seemed relieved. "I was a-feared you'd try to tell me he was a no-account and try to give him to me again. I don't want to cheat you none, and I'll pay a fair price."

I nodded profoundly, because that seemed the safest.

"I come prepared," Jed's dad said. "None of my folks ever had no high-bred bird dog, but I got money in my pocket that's more money as I ever heard of anybody paying for a dog back home."

He held out the money in a hand I noticed was clean and blue with cold. There were eight five-dollar bills and ten ones.

I hesitated judiciously, then took it. "It's a fair price for him," I said, and I guess it was.

"Done," Jed's father said, and relaxed suddenly. I didn't realize how tense he'd been.

"You know," he confided, "this'll make a mighty fine Christmas at our place. I was feelin' kind of poorly, because that's about what we had set aside for Christmas presents, and no matter what we got Jed, it wouldn't of been no good to him, and that would of made it no good for us. This way the old woman and me get a Christmas present for nothing."

I got Brute's registry out of the file and signed the transfer, then put on my coat, and we walked down the path to the kennel. It was crisp and clearing up now, and the people in the house were singing carols.

In the anonymous intimacy of darkness, Jed's dad said, "It ain't no wise fittin' for a boy to cry himself to sleep on Christmas Eve."

"Well," I said, "it's a hard world. A boy has to learn."

"It don't hurt none for him to learn a little at a time," Jed's dad said. "I'm purely sentimental that way."

"Me, too," I said.

The door swung open, and the dog who was the fruit of all the years since Mohawk and Gladstone, and who was worth every cent of fifty dollars, came out quietly, and the two of them walked down the drive in the eerie shadowed light of winter night in the woods. I thought how I would remember Brute with a warmth that does not remain for some dogs who were better and braver and who tried harder to be good for me. Brute was a kind of prodigal. He took away a cherished theory about how you can find some good in any dog, and then he gave it back, all proved up to date — just in time for Christmas.

Jack Kulpa *was born on the South Side of Milwaukee, at what was then the edge of town. He grew up along the Root River before moving to northern Wisconsin. This eventually led to life in a wilderness cabin, the first of several that he and his wife, Peggy, have built. They live with their son, Nick, on Lake Superior. A regular contributor to magazines like* Field & Stream, *Jack has won awards for outdoor writing, and his work appears in anthologies and films. An avid duck hunter and fisherman, he prefers places "beyond the reach of roads." He believes sportsmanship is another word for good manners and that ethics — or the lack of them — will decide the future of sportsmen.*

Reprinted by permission of the author.
This story first appeared in Field & Stream *magazine in 1991.*

Just One More

JACK KULPA

There are many ways to while away
a long Wisconsin winter. Yet I am
never ready to surrender grouse season,
never ready to accept winter and
its ruthless finality.

*I*n my corner of Wisconsin, grouse season ends on New Year's Eve, but most bird hunters hang up their guns long before Thanksgiving. By then, deep snow has closed the logging trails and thickets, and travel is a matter of snowshoes and skis. Besides, everyone knows the best hunting takes place in October, before the year's young birds have been shot at and dispersed. Yet the last days of the season may bring the most memorable shooting. Certainly, they help make a long winter a bit easier to endure.

In the North, winter may arrive any time in November, when hunting shacks are vacant and shuttered and no one is abroad in the land to disrupt the feeling of solitude and isolation. The frozen earth lies rigid, every lake is locked in ice, and the bare branches of aspens weave a stark tracery against the sky. Everything is ready for the coming of the snow.

One morning in November I left the cabin to find the woods gripped in a hush. In the air was a breathless expectation, a sense of waiting and watching as the gray sky filled with clouds. Gone now were the small, dry rustlings of autumn, the chatter of red squirrels and the calls of chickadees. The quiet lay like a crushing weight on everything, a prelude to the silences that winter would bring.

I wanted to try for one more bird before the storm broke and winter changed the pace of life. I headed for a tamarack swamp along a chain of tiny lakes. At the edge of the muskeg where the land began to rise, ruffed grouse would be lying in the laurel and dogwood. Dry leaves crackled like cellophane as I walked downhill toward the swamp. The grouse were anxious and alert to every sound; I could hear birds flushing far ahead of me.

But things improved when I reached the heather. Though starched with frost, the muskeg's mat was still soft and spongy, and by walking its edge I could move without a sound. Now the birds bolted from the hillside, close enough to hit with a rock. I stopped to rest after an hour, and to admire the two birds tucked in my vest. Only then did I notice the muted rustling. Not a blade of grass quivered, not a leaf fluttered, and everywhere was a soft whispering. It was snowing, and in a moment the air was white with drifting flakes. Down they came, speckling the earth, clinging to rocks and logs until the brown earth was no longer merely mottled, but solidly cloaked in white. The woods filled quickly with wet, heavy snow. Visibility decreased as the flakes floated down, obliterating landmarks. The quiet was complete now, the calm profound. Autumn with its riotous color and excitement was over. Winter had returned to the North.

A month later, twenty inches of snow lay on the ground. No longer were the grasses showing, or the stiff, sere stems of asters and weeds. Windfalls and stumps were completely covered, and in open places the earth was a smooth, white expanse. Balsams and spruces were heavily laden; slender birches were bending low. It was always cold, and one morning I awoke to find sundogs blazing on the horizon. After breakfast, I took the gun and snowshoes and broke trail along a logging road. In an aspen copse I found where the birds had been at work; their tracks were everywhere among the trees, and in a rosy clump of sumac where they had fed on seeds. Wing marks showed where grouse had plunged into snowbanks to spend the nights; I kicked open one drift and found an empty, ice-encrusted bed. With so much evidence, I was sure the birds were nearby. As the sun rose and warmed the day, they would break out of their burrows to feed on aspen buds.

The first grouse burst from a snowbank at the edge of the aspens. It took me by surprise, and all I could do was watch its wild, twisting flight through the trees. Then two more exploded like firecrackers from a drift. The first bird streaked ahead toward a ridge and was almost to the rise when I dropped it; the other flew behind me, hurtling through space for the balsams at my back. I turned from the waist and fired, amazed to see the grouse tumble into the snow.

I picked up the birds and turned toward home. Any other shooting I might find would be anticlimactic. I had made a double on grouse, the first in many seasons. It seemed a fine way to end the year. To be sure, there are many ways to while away a long Wisconsin winter. There are rabbits to chase, squirrels to hunt, and even time enough to take a second deer with a bow. There are walleyes to catch, sturgeon to spear, and beneath the ice of Lake Superior the trout will be biting. Yet for all that, I am never ready to surrender grouse season, never ready to accept winter and its ruthless finality. The end of the year means more than snow, cold and ice. It also means that time is growing shorter.

So it was that on New Year's Eve I went back into the woods. There was time to take one more bird before the season ended, and it seemed wrong not to make the most of that. It was twenty below, and the only sound in the icy silence was the creak of my snowshoes as I shuffled over the crust of the trail where I had made the double.

On a distant ridge the setting sun was a quivering globe of vermilion; as it sank it drained all color from the sky. The tote road weaved its way through a stark and barren country, a land of black spruce, gray birch and white snow. There was no stirring, no rustling, no hint of sound or movement. Life had changed in the North; its pulse was weak, and barely felt. Staying alive was the only aim of every creature, and only the strongest would survive until spring, when the ridges would tremble again with the sound of drumming grouse.

On both sides of the trail white birches stood like picked bones. A gust of wind rattled the trees, accentuating the silence. The sun was setting quickly and darkness was rushing in. I stepped up on the crest of a drift, and when I did a big partridge burst like a bomb from the snow. It sent me reeling, and I would have lost sight of the bird had it flown any distance; but it only sailed into the top of a birch and began to bud, unconcerned. It was an easy shot and no one was looking; but it would have been a terrible way to end the year.

The bird tottered precariously on the high, lithe branches, losing its balance at times but keeping itself aloft with frantic wingbeats. As I watched, a last, level ray of sunlight struck the birch tops. When it did, the purple branches all but flamed. The trunks of the trees glistened like silver rapiers; even the grouse appeared dazzling in the light — the dull, brown bird now gleamed like amber. In a world where all elements were intent on crushing survival, the grouse was a testament to quiet perseverance.

The image lasted only an instant. The sun fell away, and darkness flooded in. The grouse lost its luster and flew away into the timber. I never raised my gun. I had gone out with the hope of bagging a bird; instead I saw a phoenix rise from a snowy tomb. Now I was ready for winter.

Also from
The Cabin Bookshelf

*These fine books are available
at your favorite bookstore.*

... of Woodsmoke
and Quiet Places

JERRY WILBER

Jerry Wilber presents a full year's worth of daily reflections on the outdoors and on life in the mythical North Country town of Lost Lake. Wilber's insights amuse and inspire, and along the way provide hints on how to be a better hunter, citizen, angler, camper, canoeist, cook, parent, spouse, friend.

400 pages   hardcover $25.95
ISBN 0-9653381-1-8

Notes From
Little Lakes

MEL ELLIS

Mel Ellis describes how he and his wife and their five daughters (The Rebels) turned a tract of pasture-land into a haven for trees, flowers, and wildlife. In the lore of nature and the environment, *Little Lakes* is as familiar and as impor-tant as Aldo Leopold's Sand County.

280 pages, hardcover
$23.95
ISBN 0-9653381-0-X

The Land,
Always the Land

MEL ELLIS

Never have the sights, sounds, and moods of the seasons been captured more vividly than in this collec-tion of writings by Mel Ellis. Ellis leads us through the year, month by month, drawing us into a world we often miss amid the swirl of daily life. After reading this book, you will see the world anew on your trips to the countryside and in your daily travels across town.

280 pages, hardcover
$23.95
ISBN 0-9653381-2-6